This coloring book is dedicated to love and
to a special person in my life whom I love and
will love until death

I0430030

Our love is like an endless story, where each chapter brings new emotions and adventures. With you, life becomes a priceless gift, and every moment spent together is a blessing.

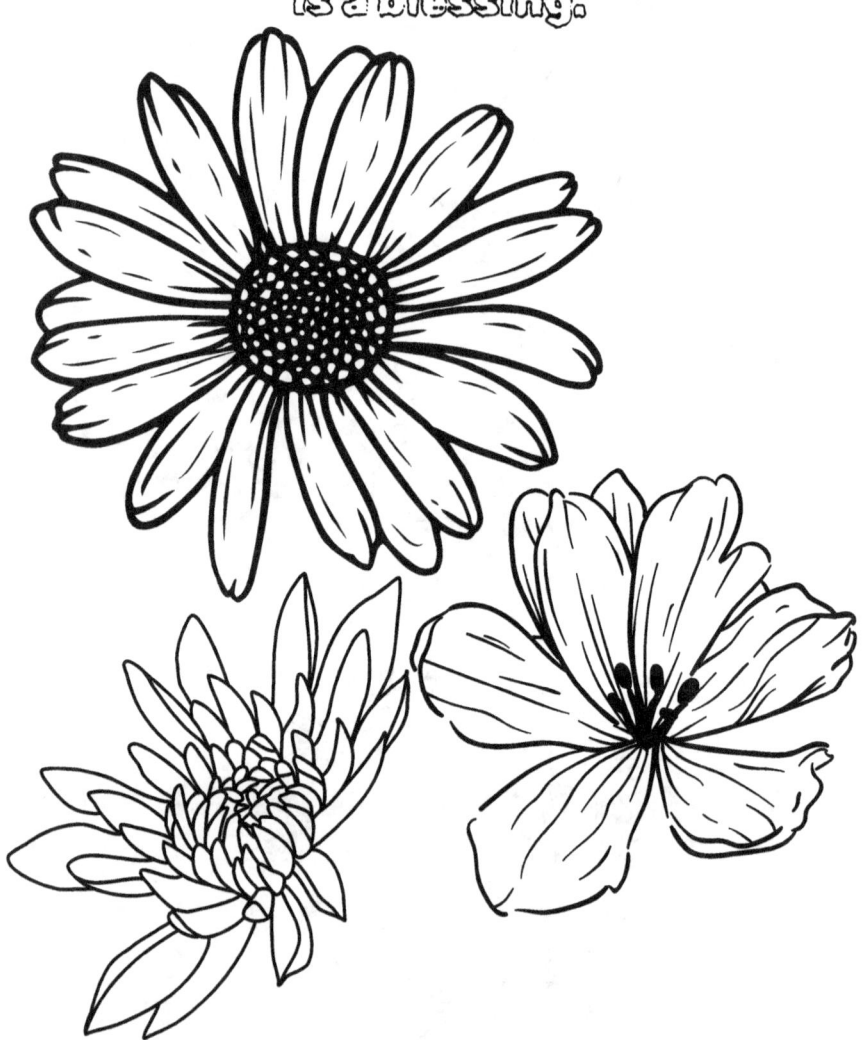

This is a coloring book with floral elements
and different designs and sizes plus many
other landscapes, birds and a fascinating
world in which to relax your mind

and a lot of funny jokes that I hope will make you smile

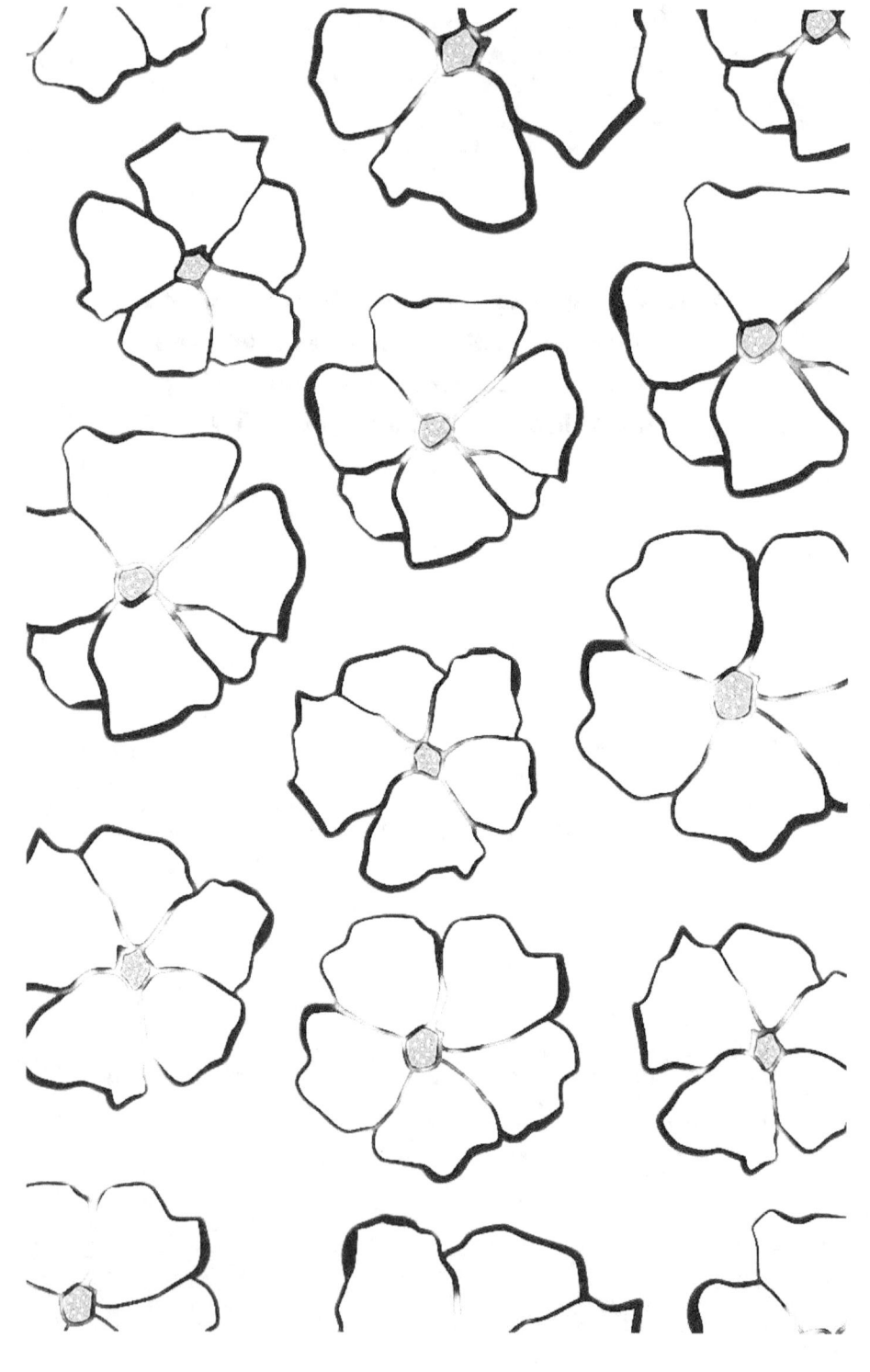

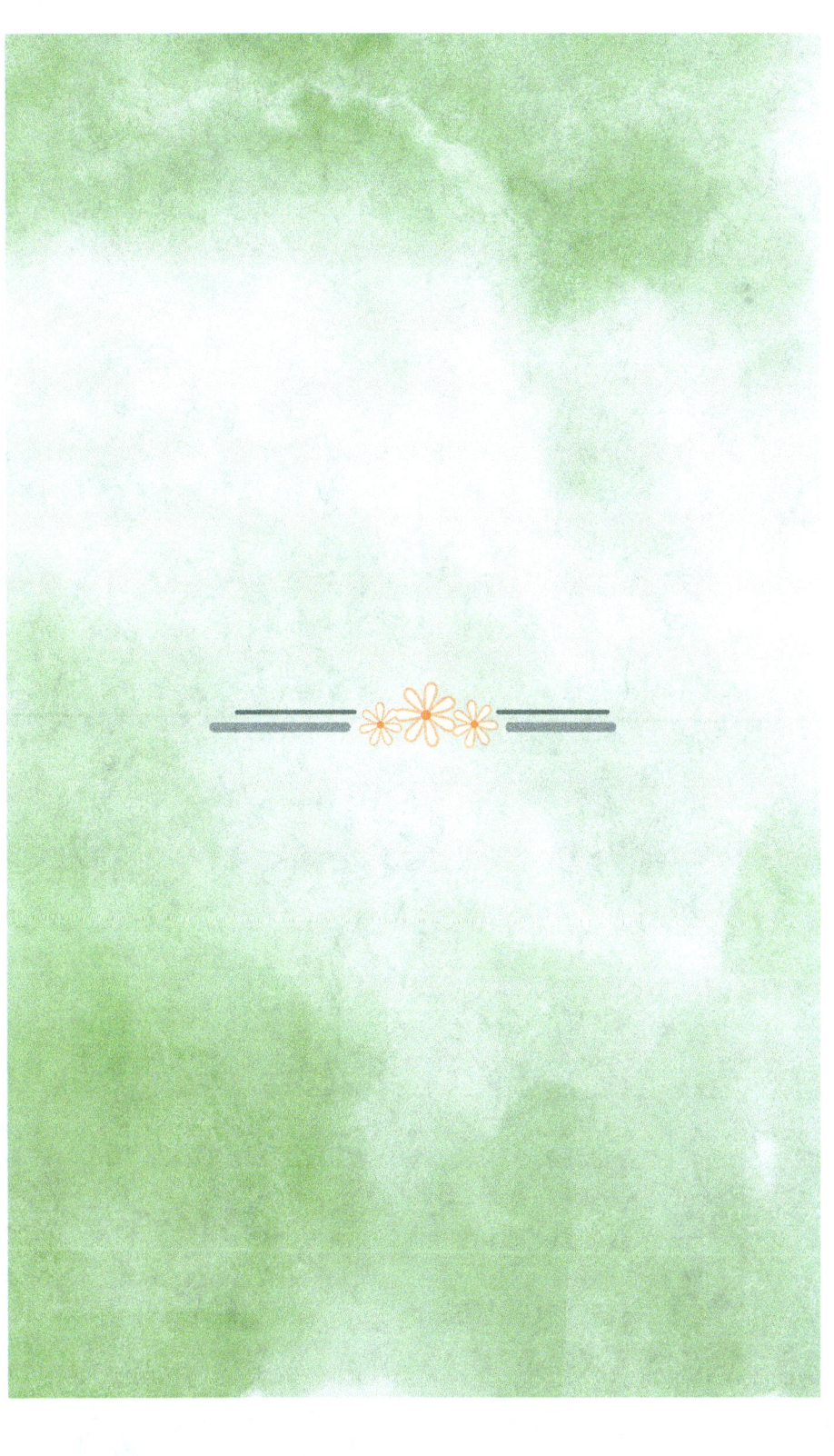

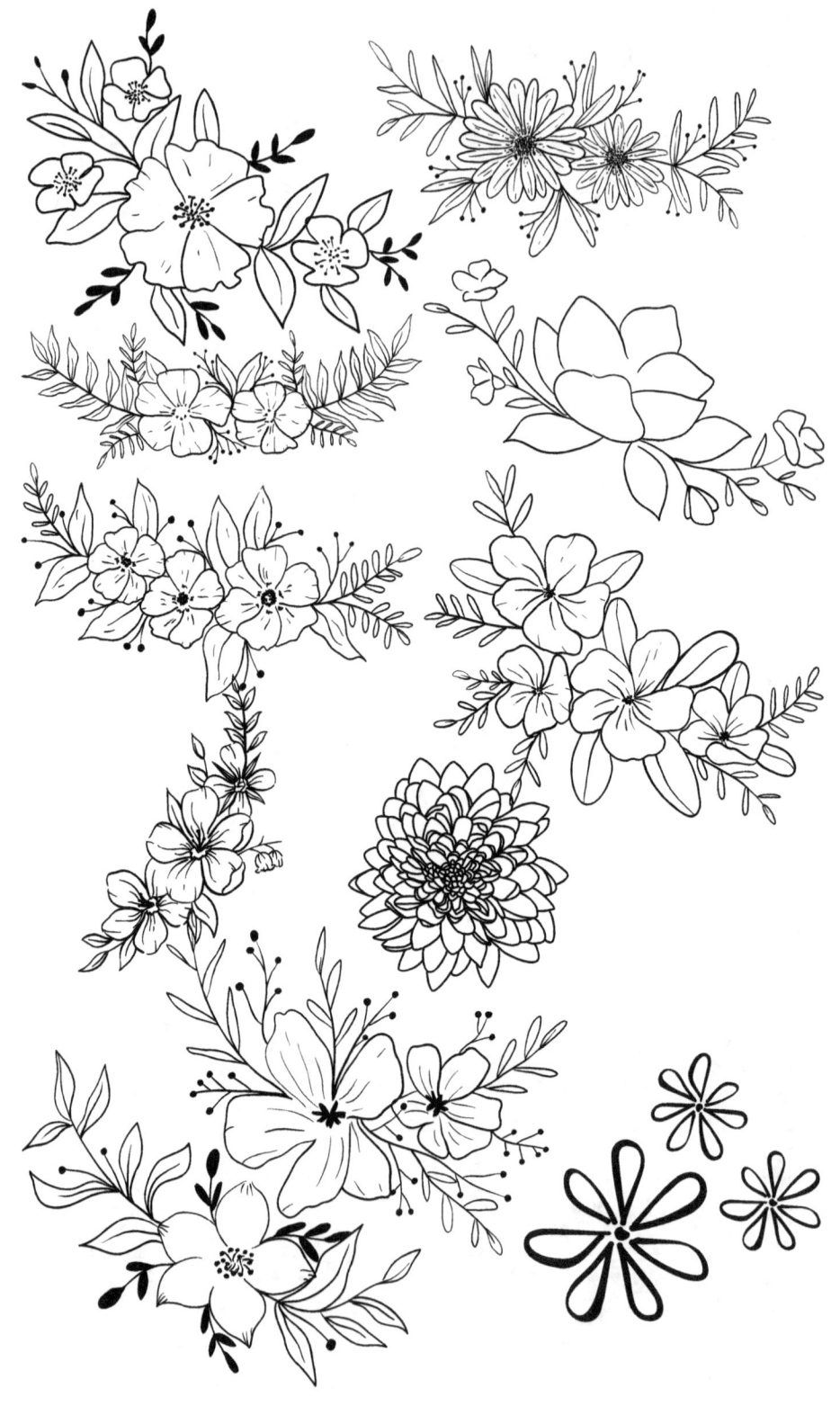

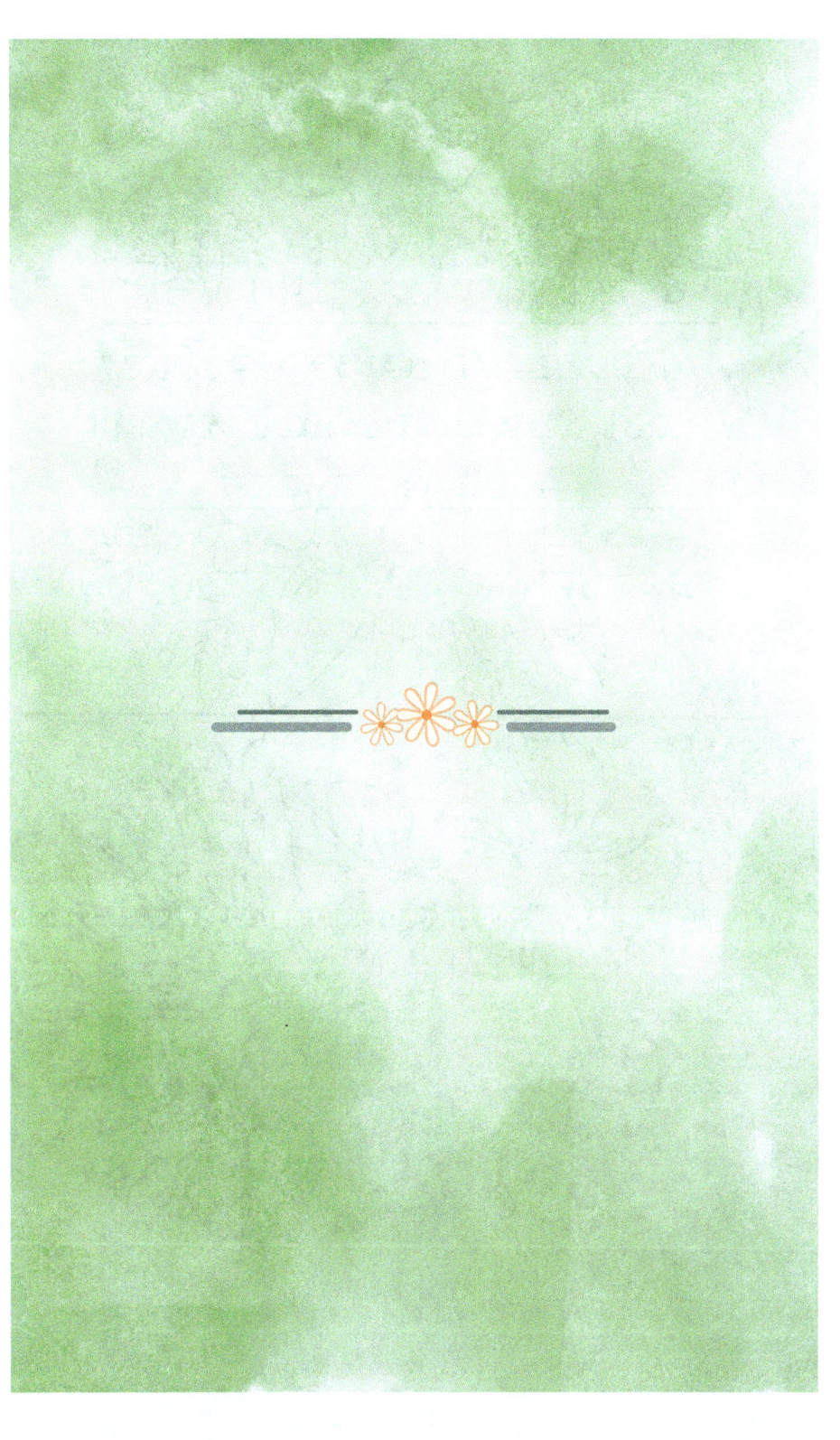

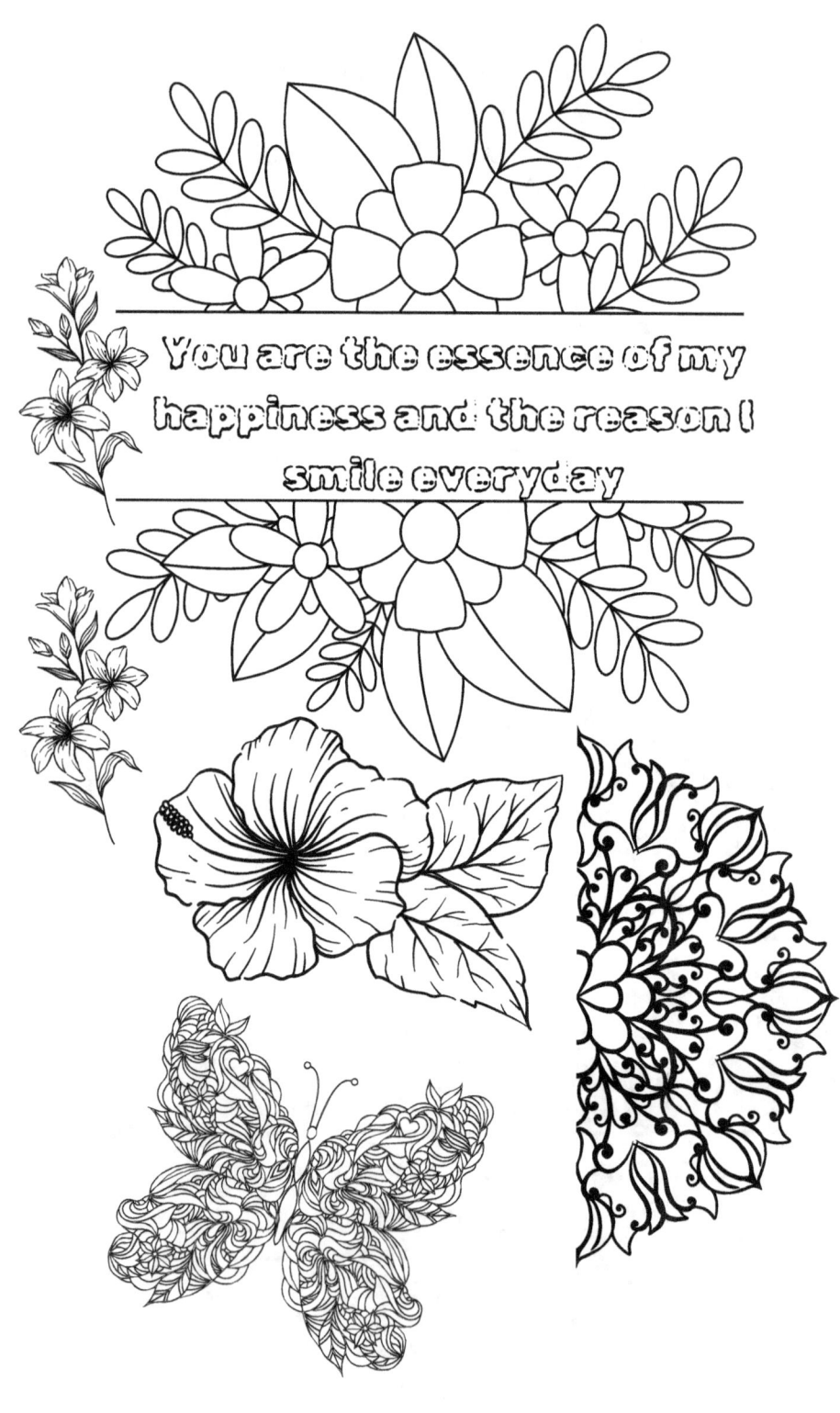

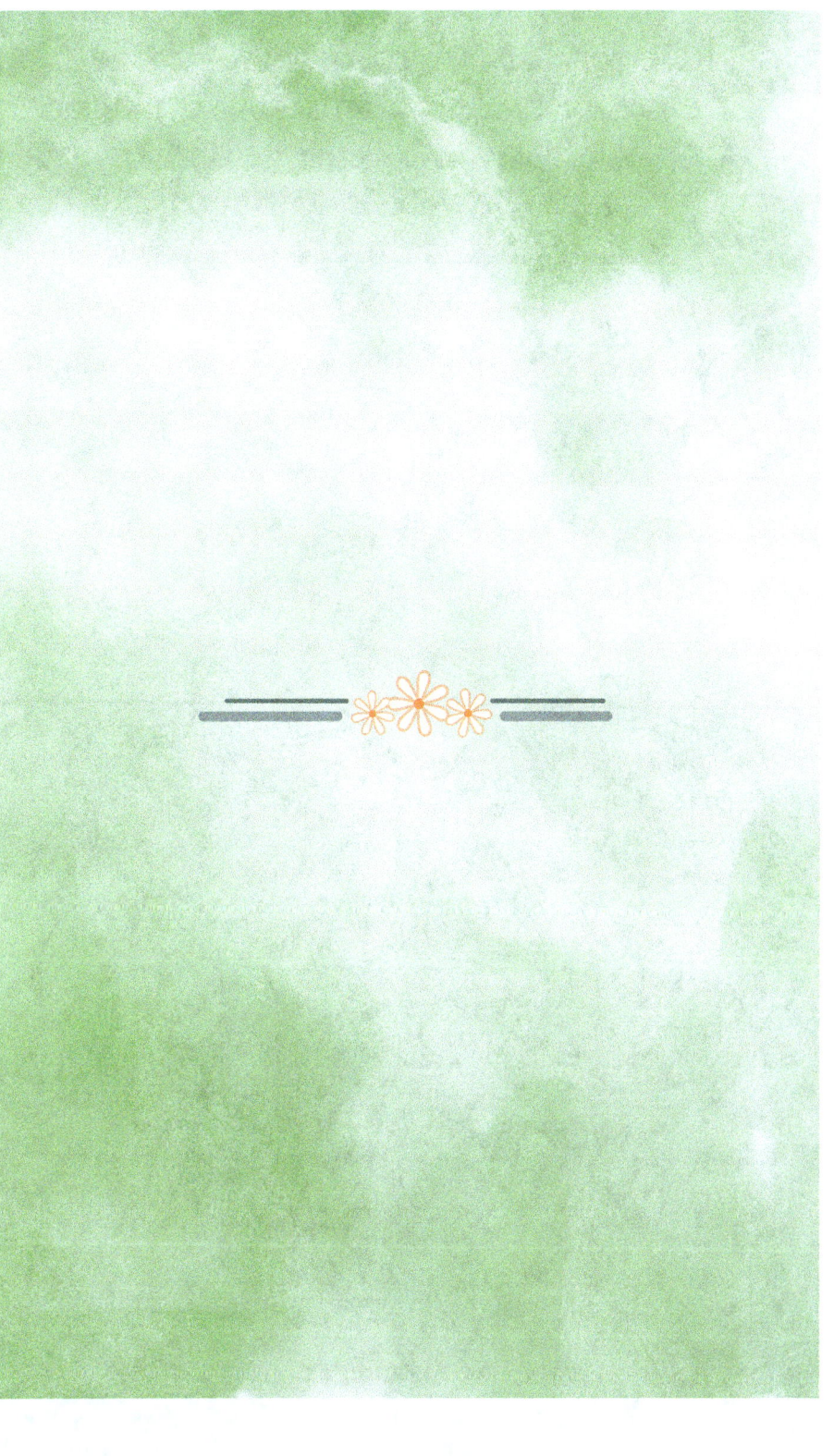

Our love is like a beacon in the midst of the storm, always lighting our way and bringing us the assurance that we will overcome any obstacle together. With you, my heart finds true peace and happiness.

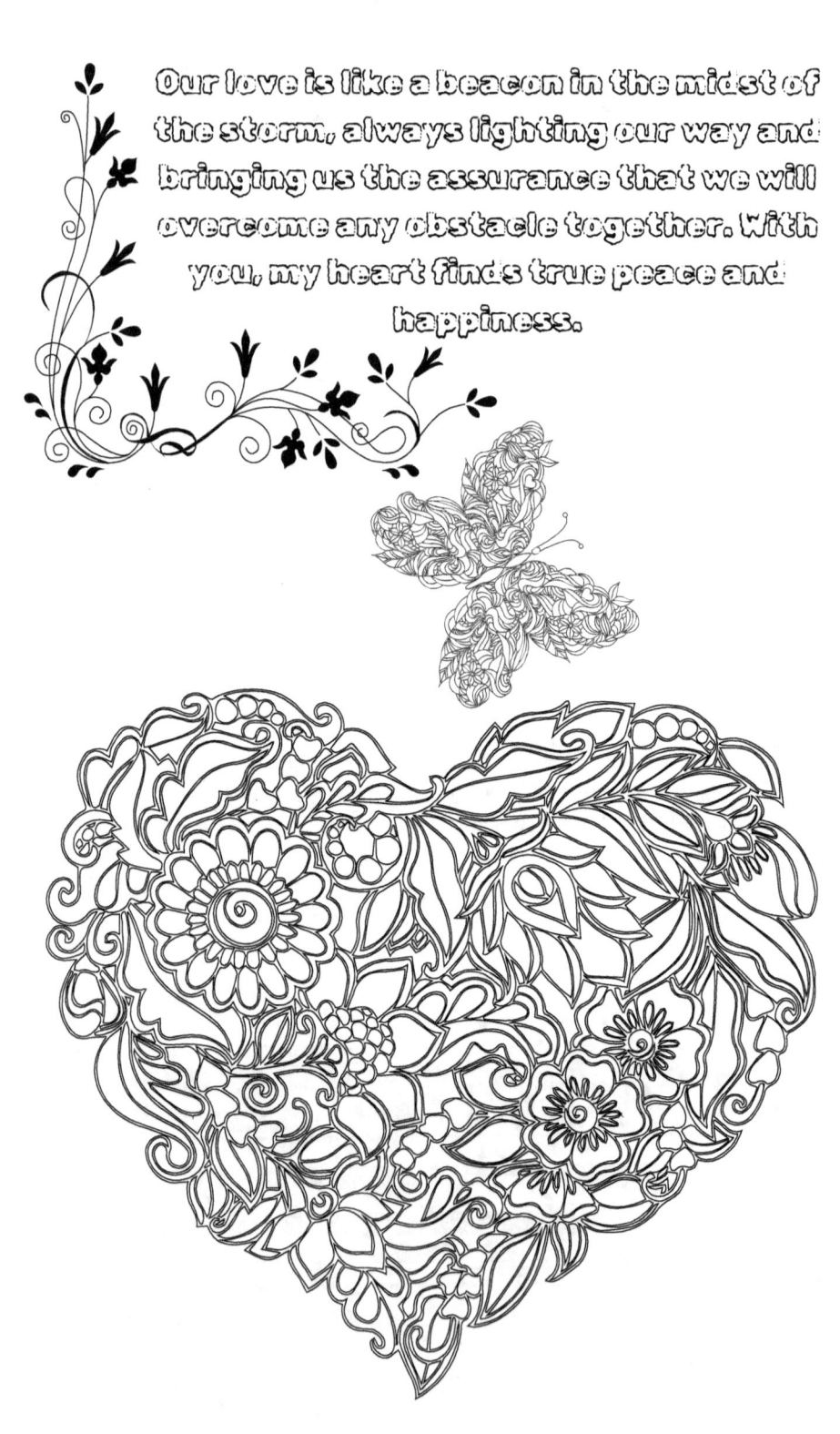

color test

find the right colors to color at a
professional level

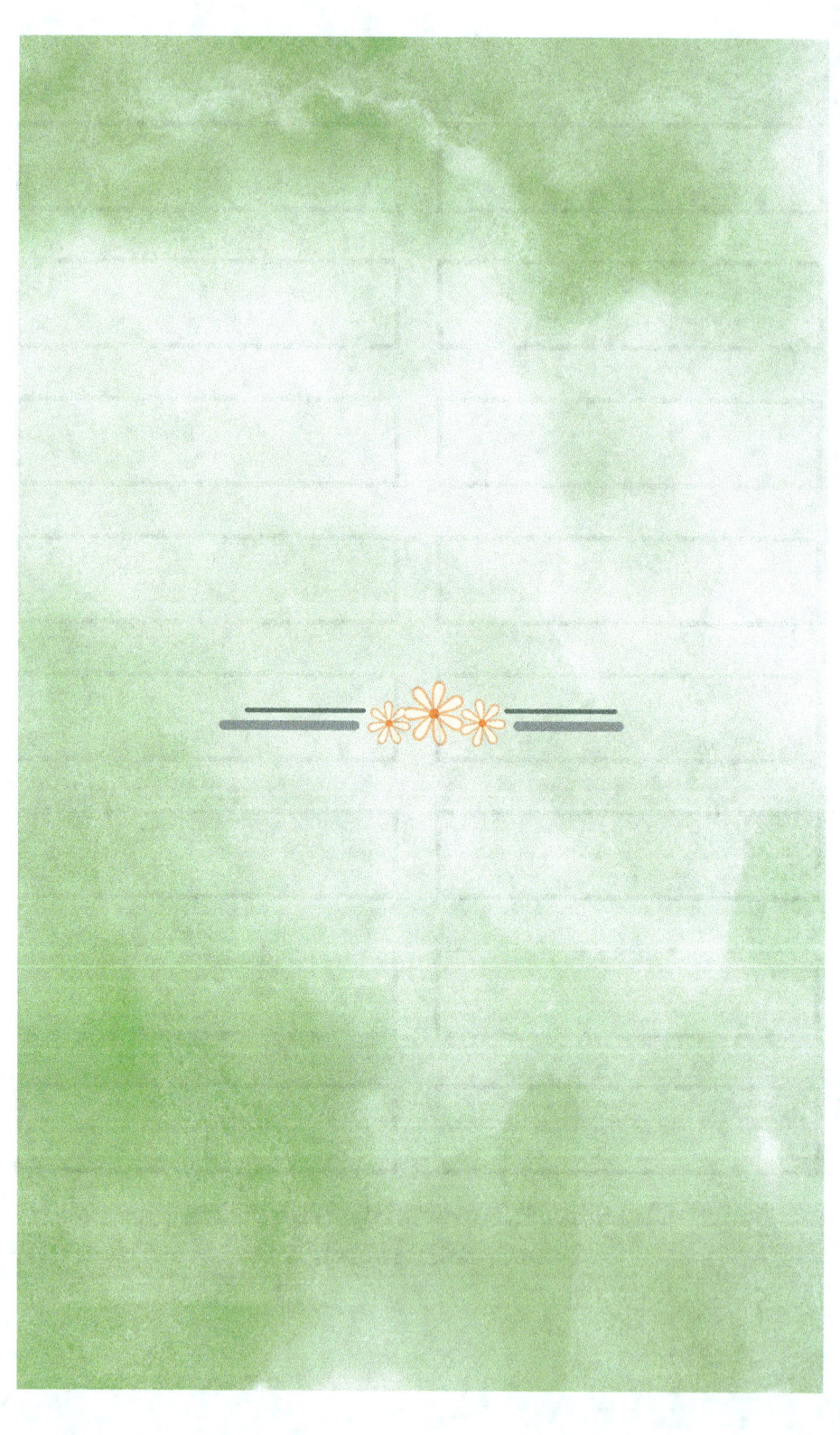

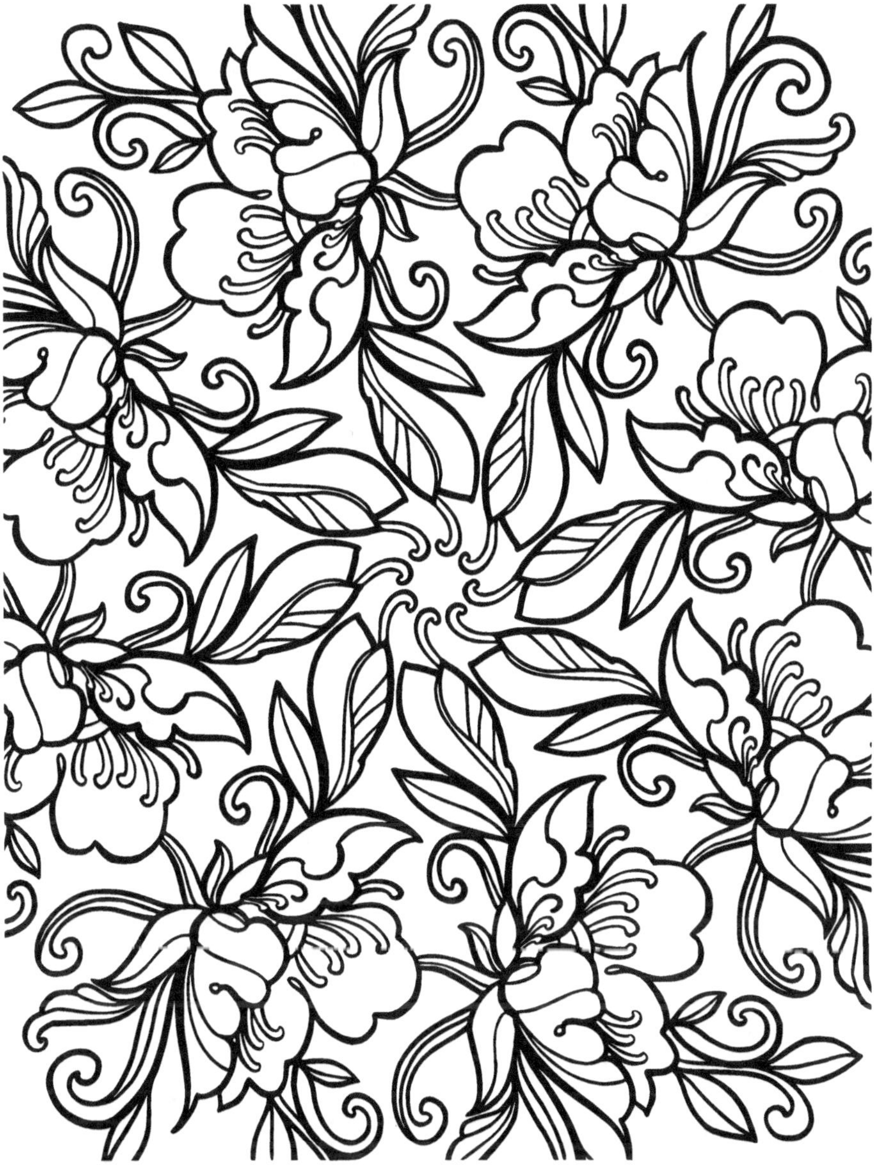

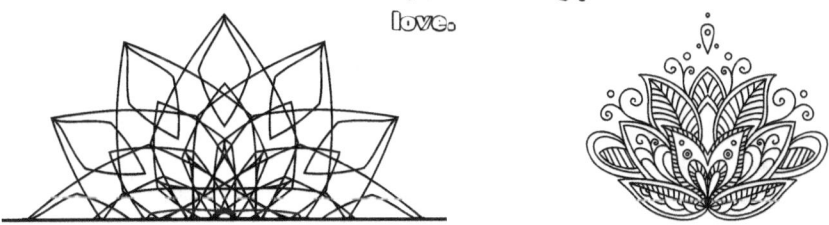

If I were a bee, you would be my favorite flower. I would fly from one flower to another, just to bring you the nectar of love.

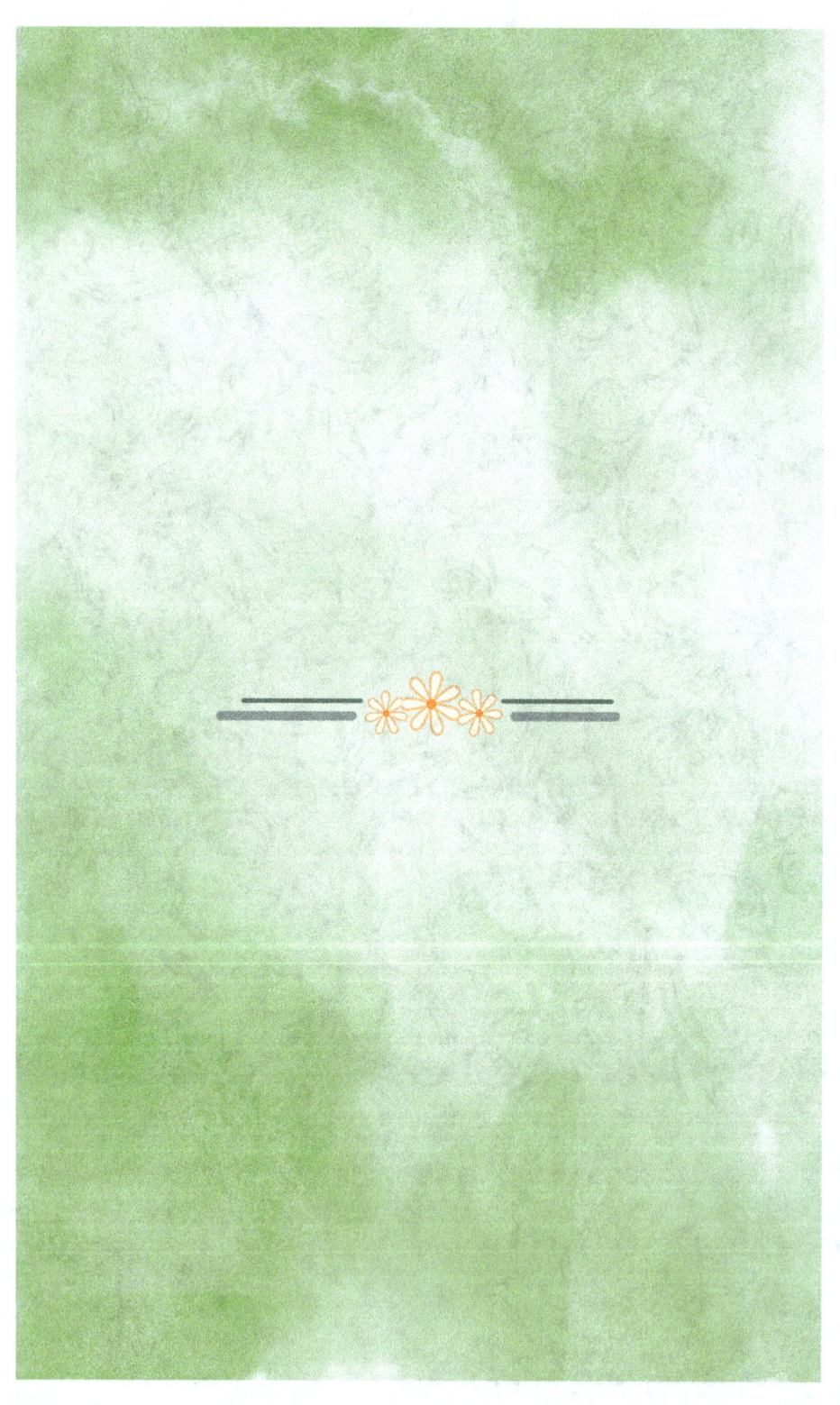

Our love is like a remote control. We could always change the channel, but I'd rather stick to your favorite show.

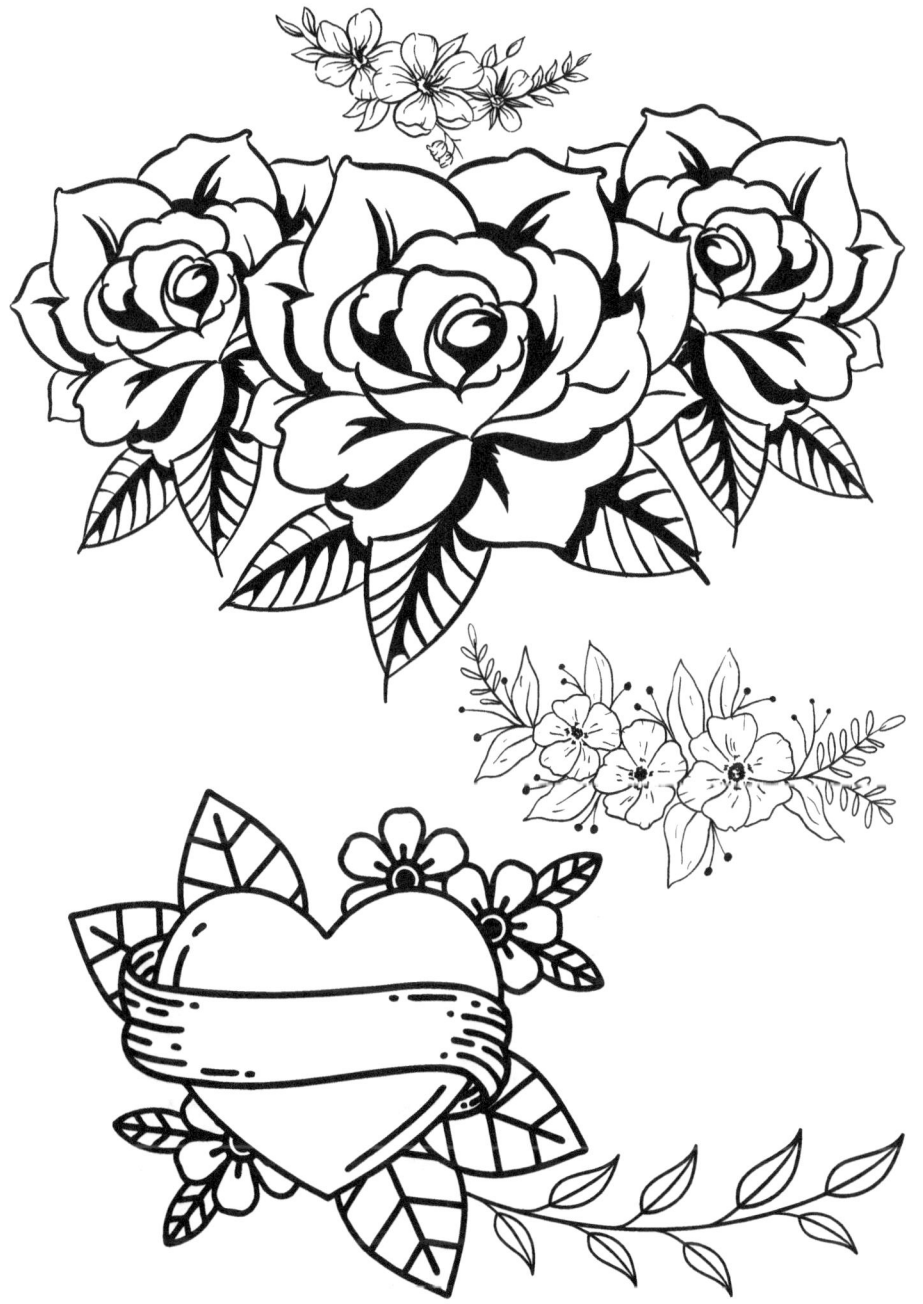

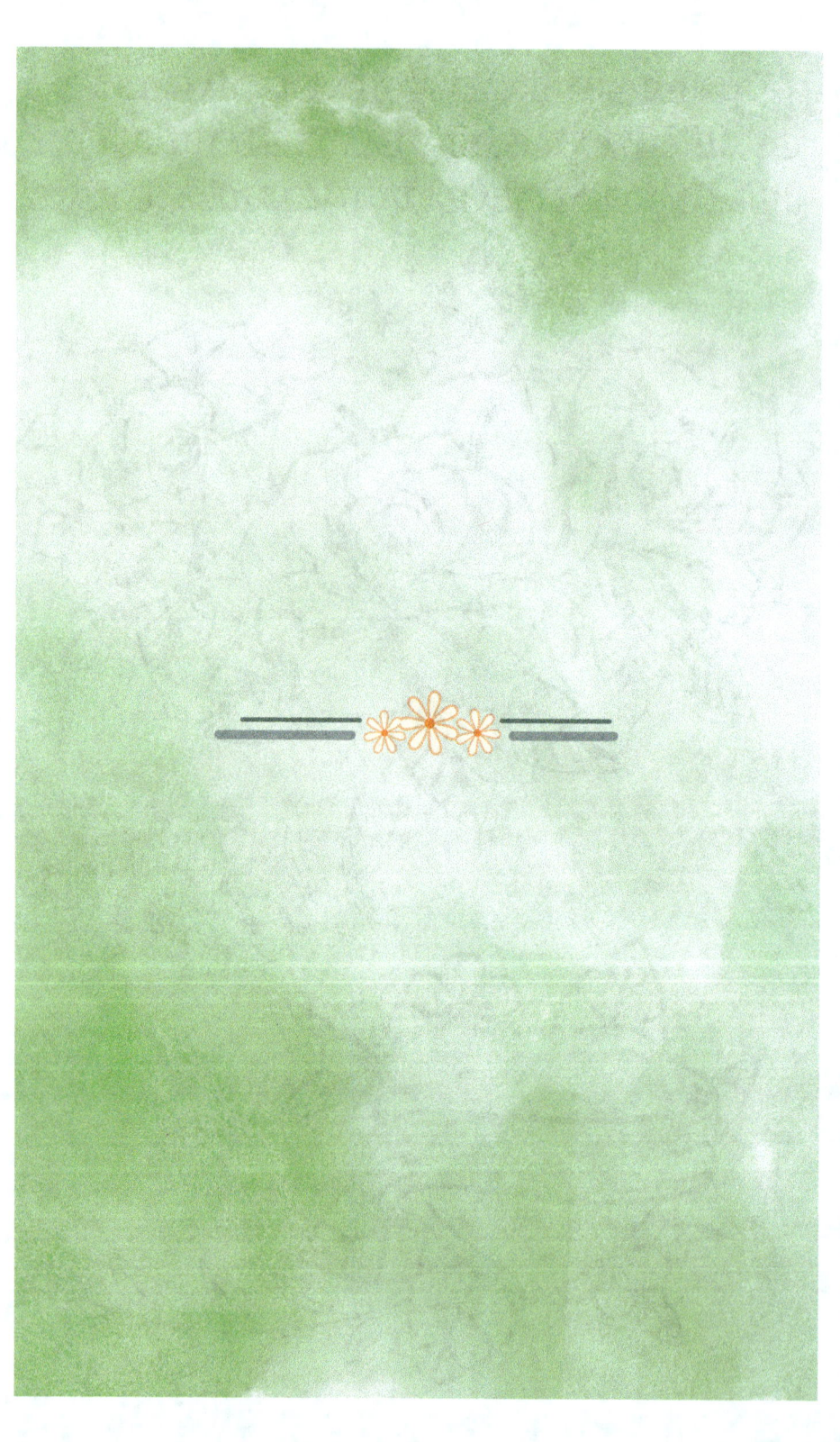

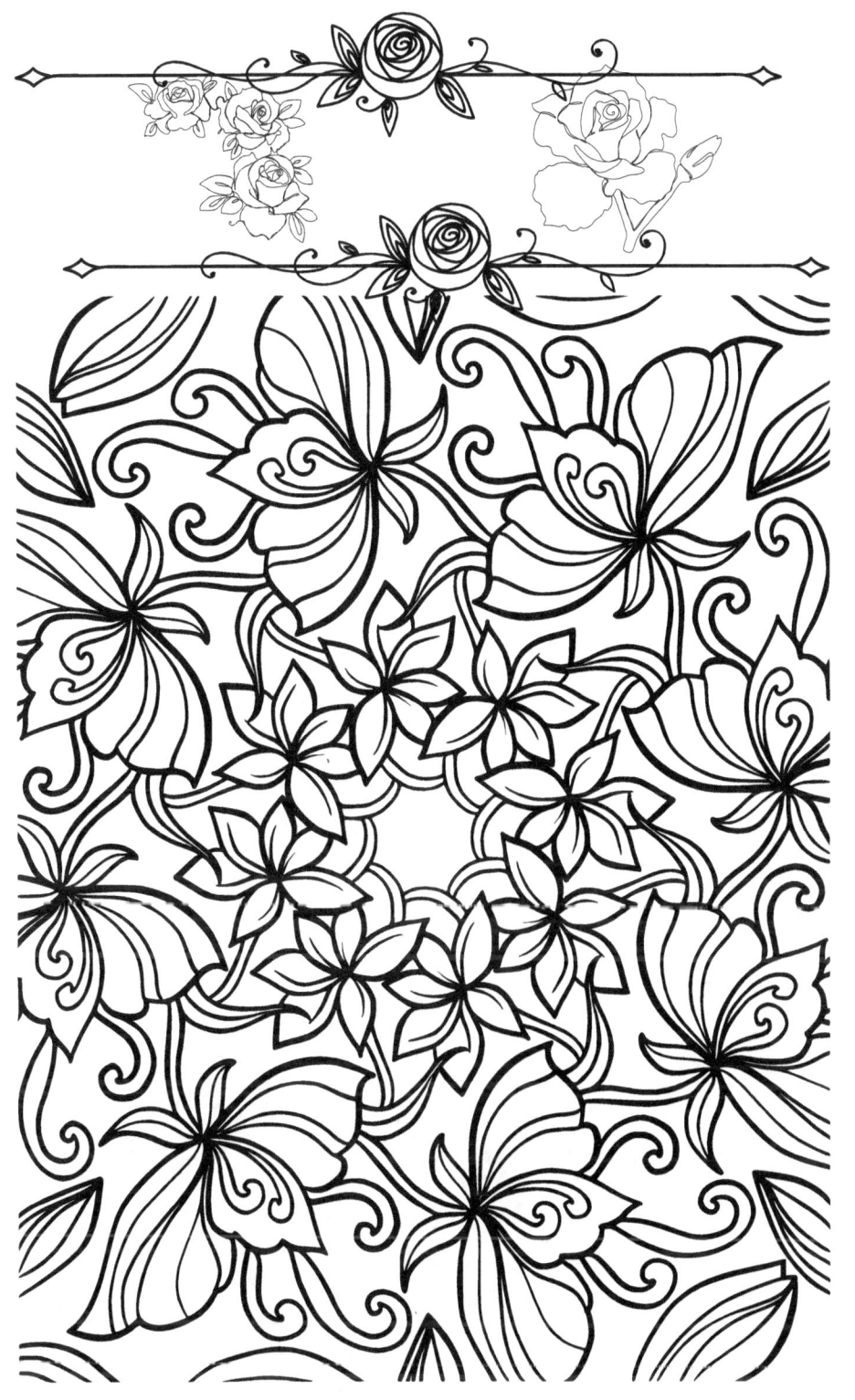

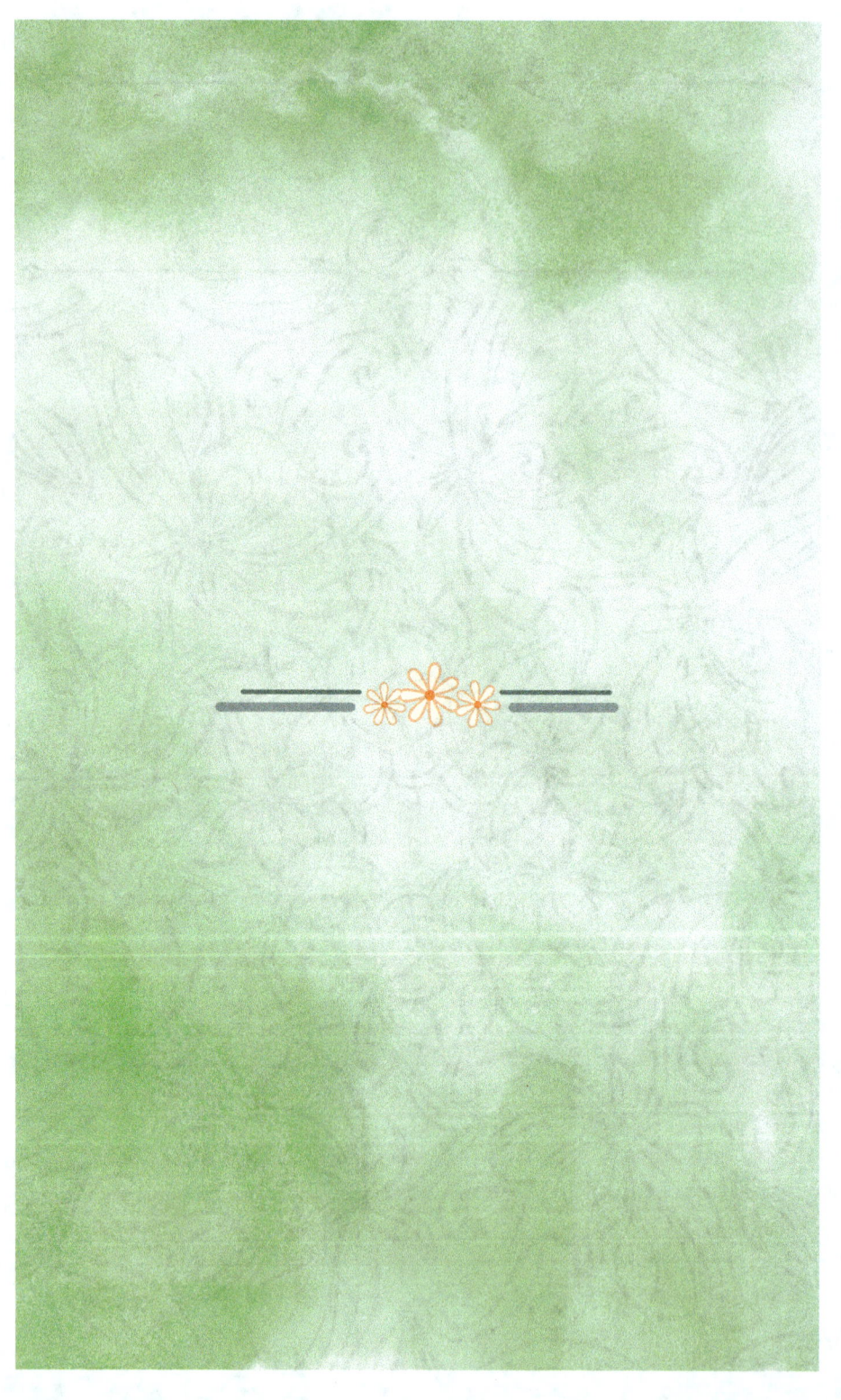

What does an astronaut do when he is bored on the ship? He takes a break and walks on his honeymoon!

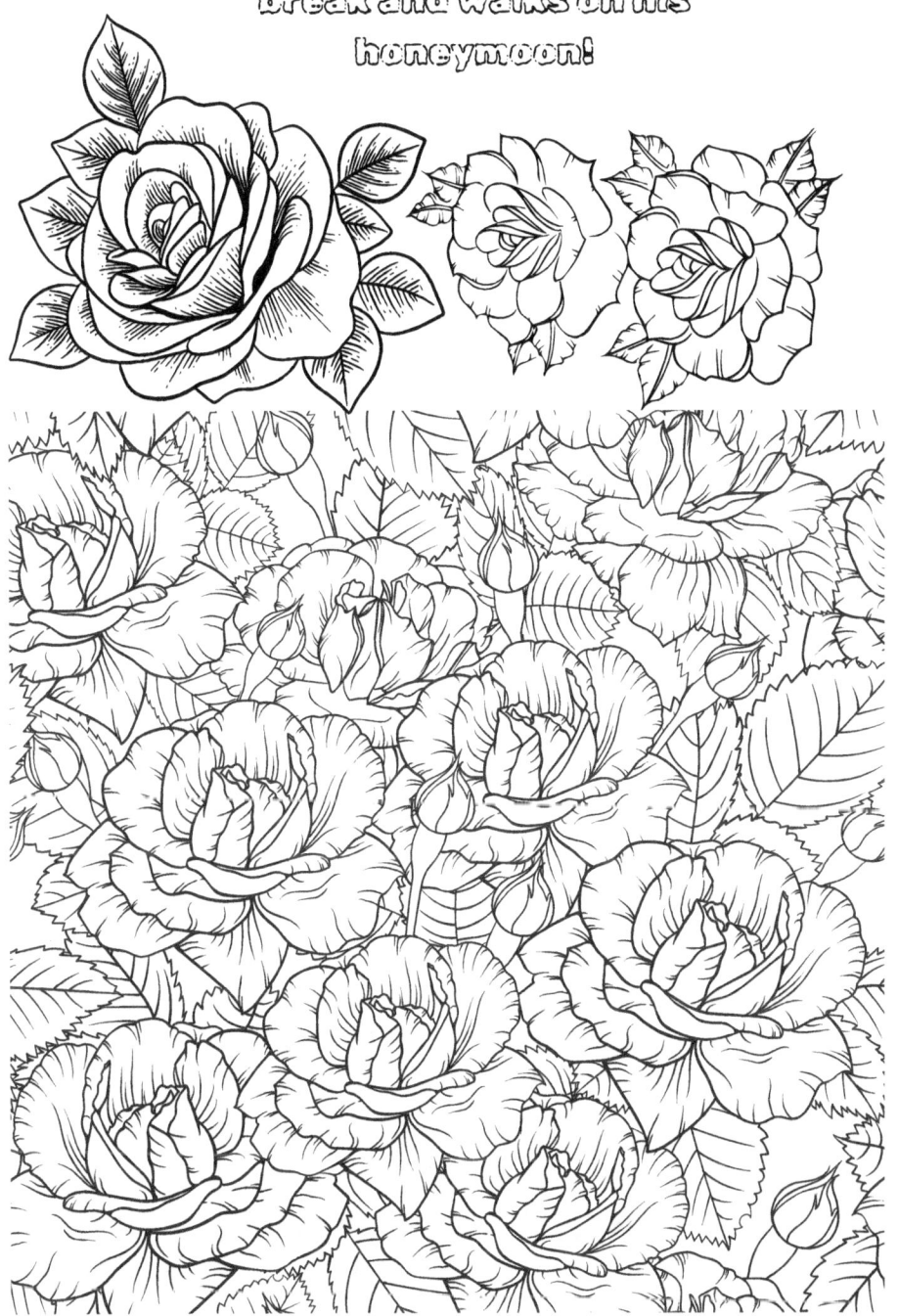

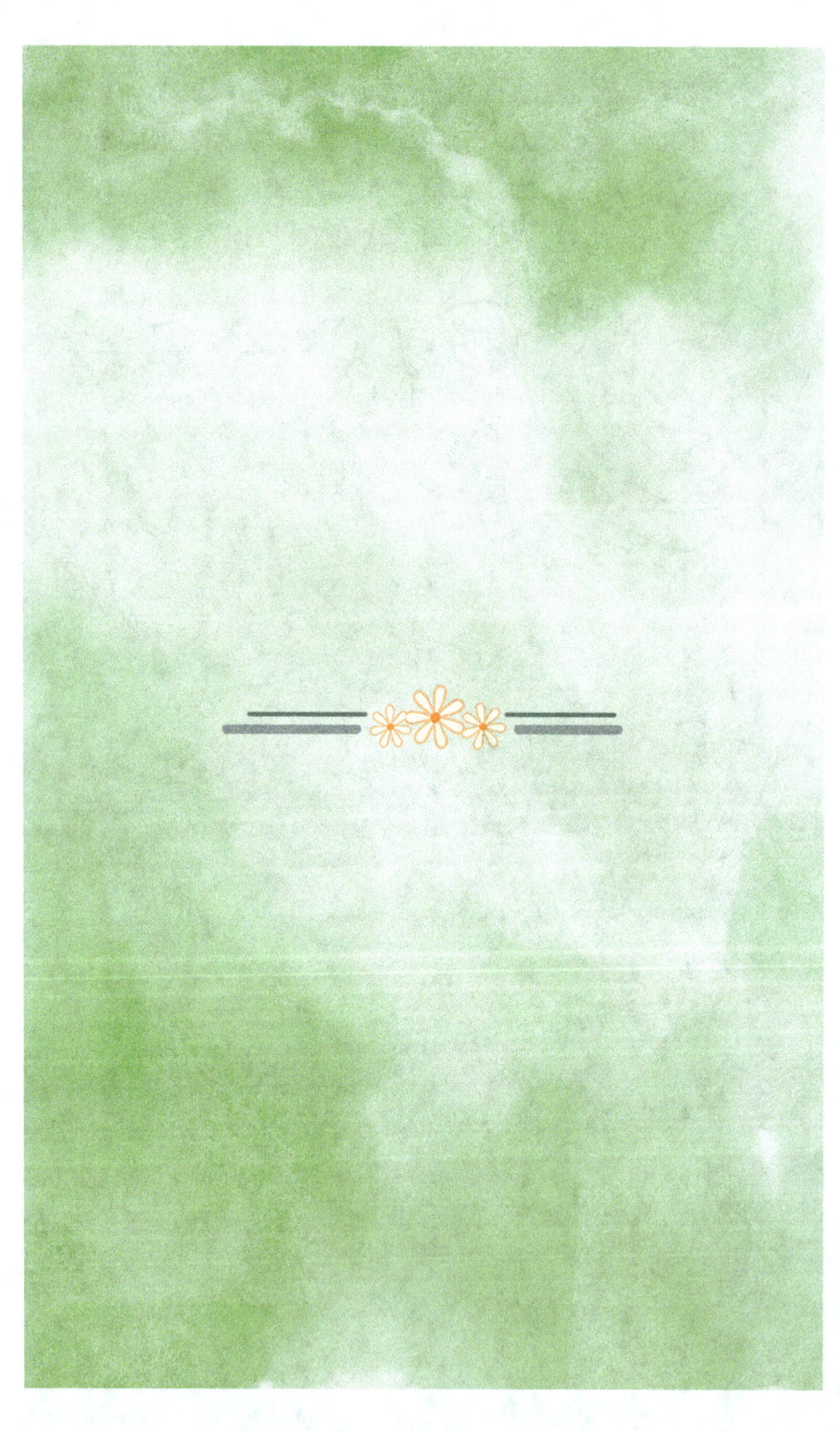

What does one pencil say to the other in a love relationship? "Without you, my world is just black and white. With you, everything takes on color!"

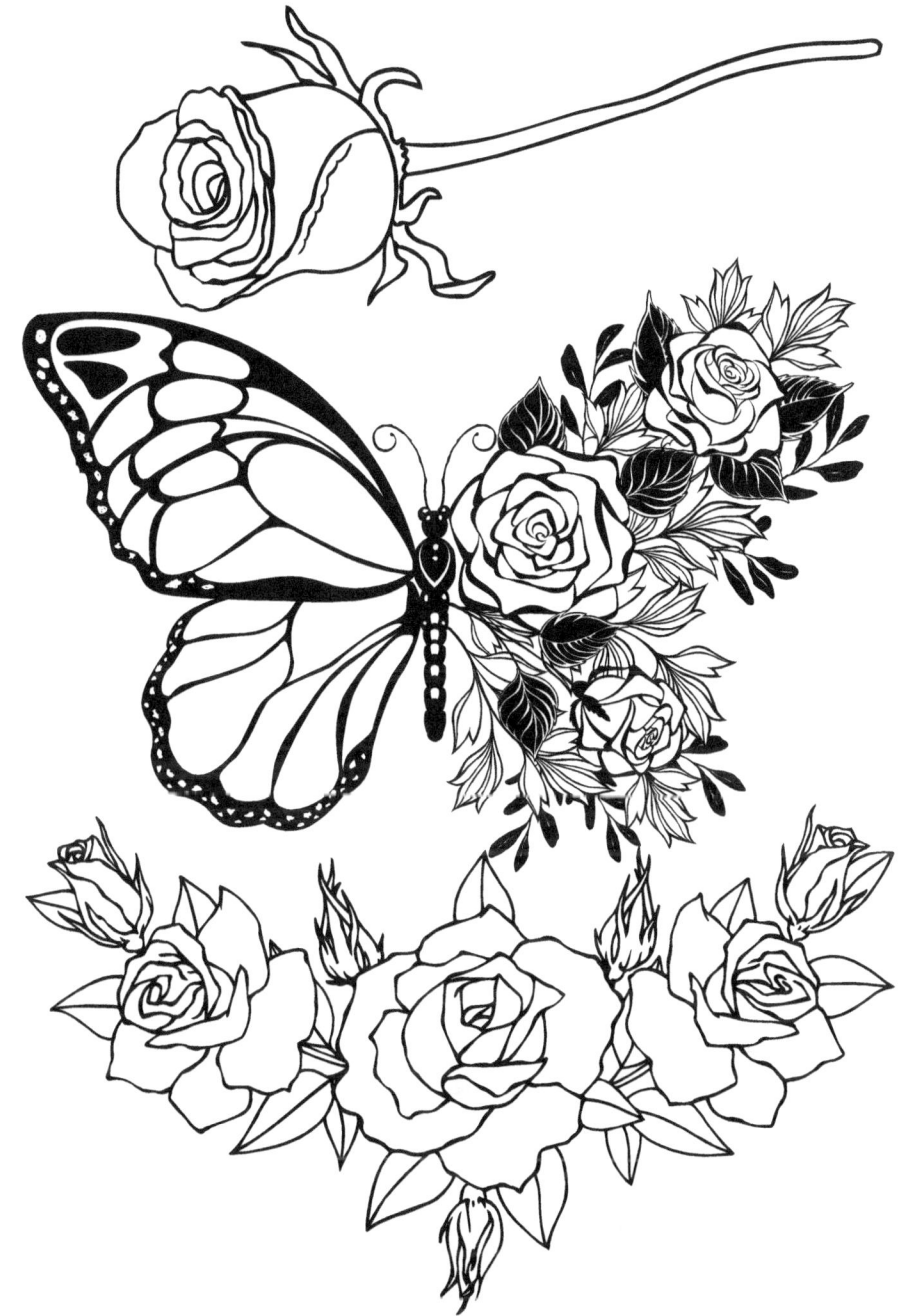

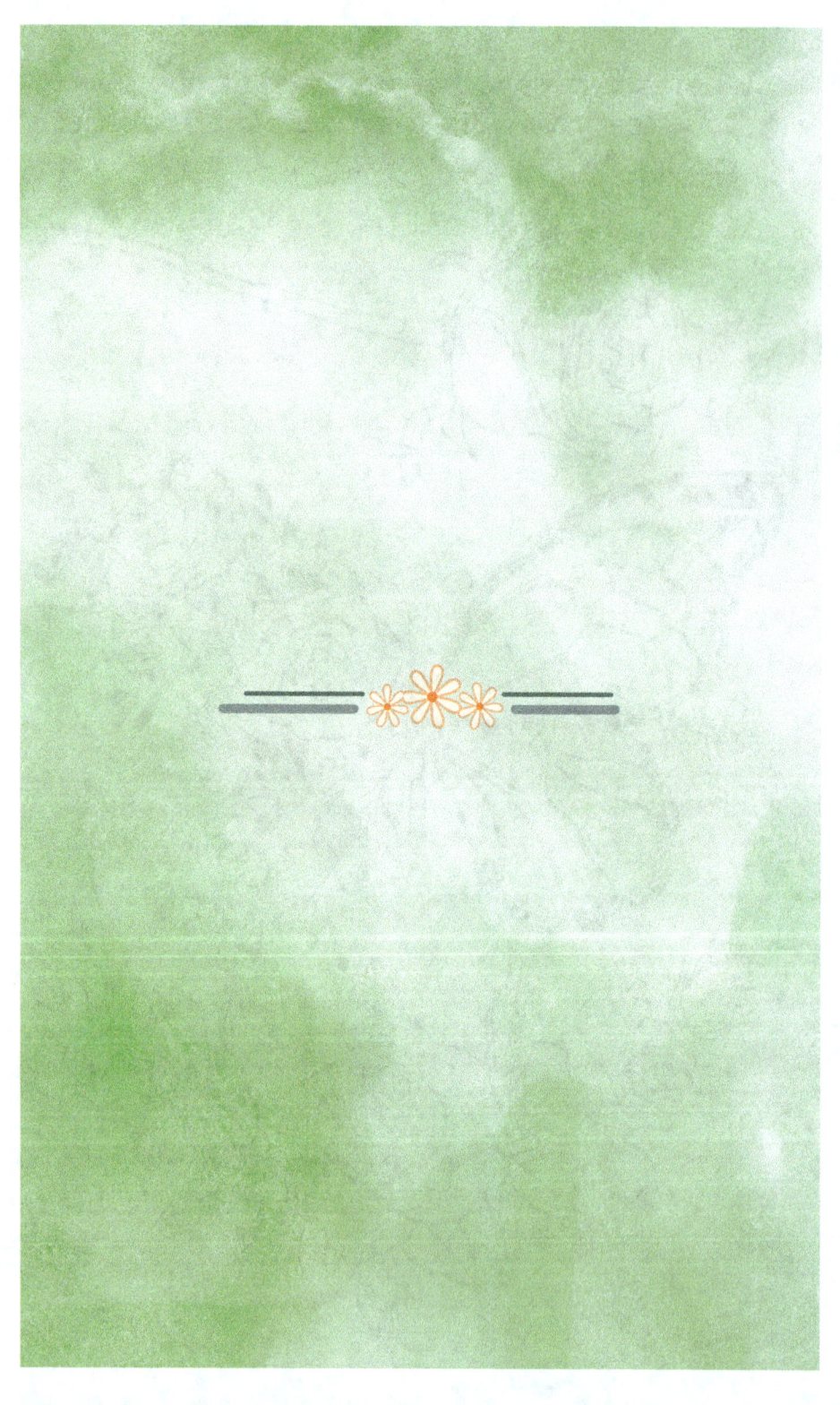

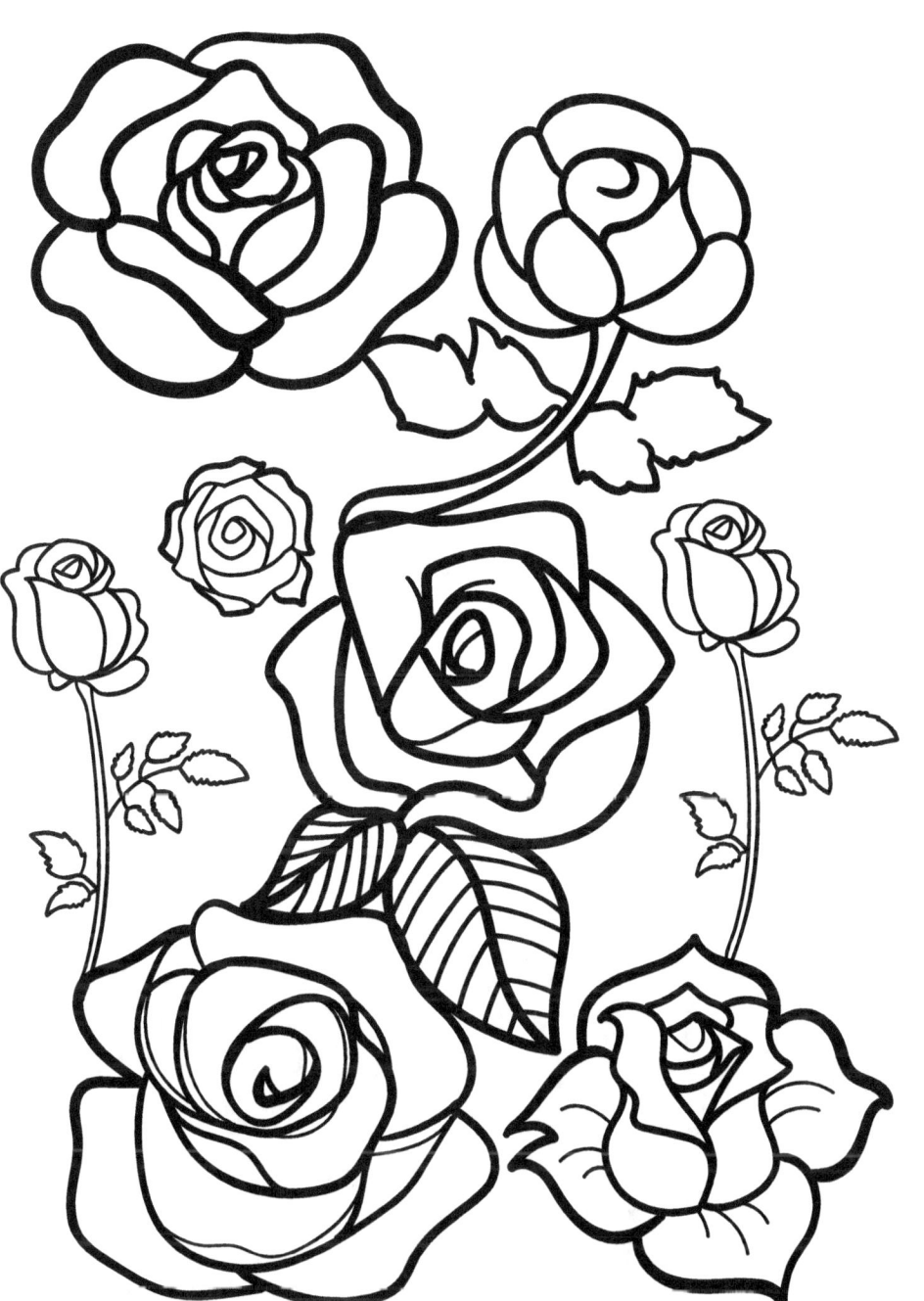

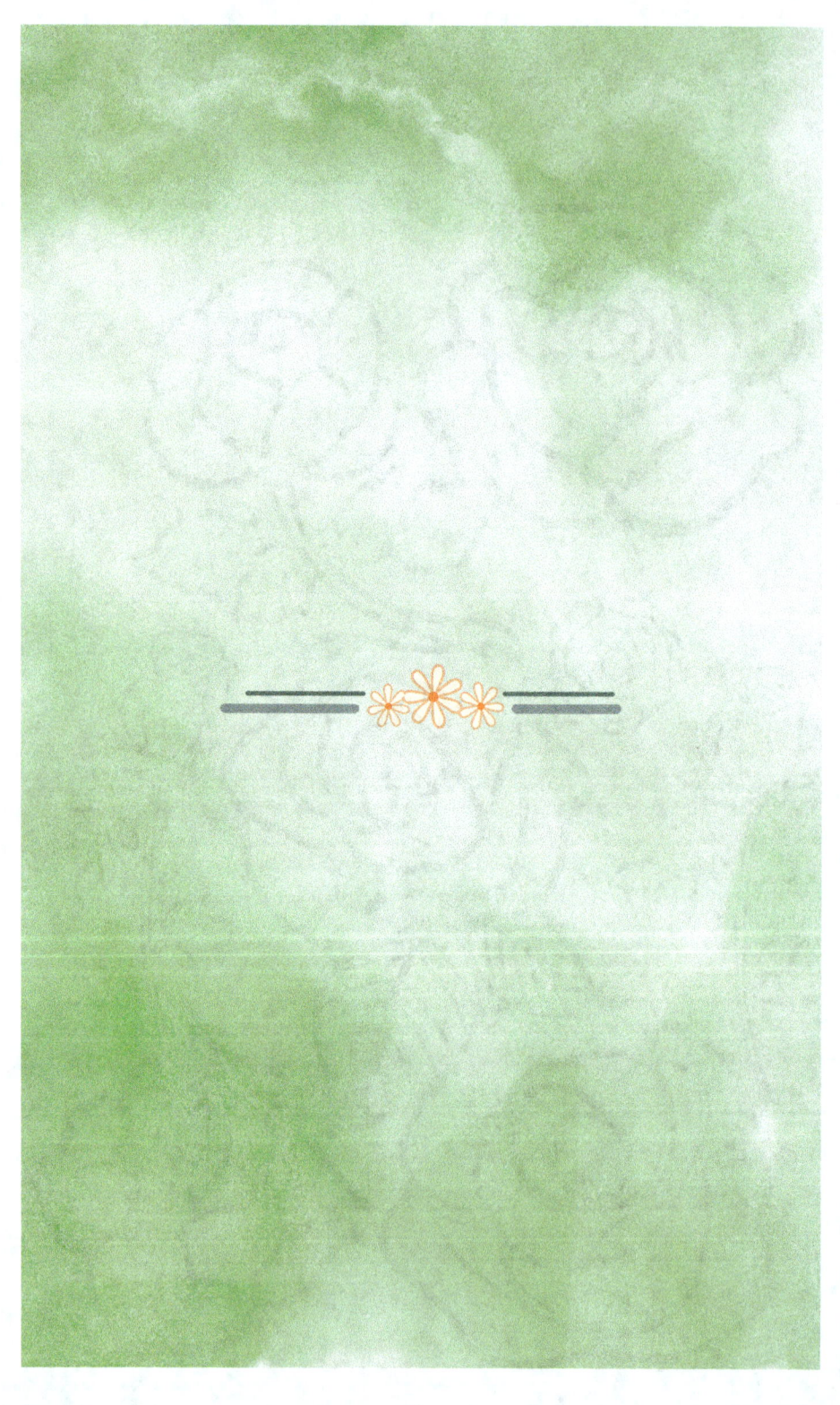

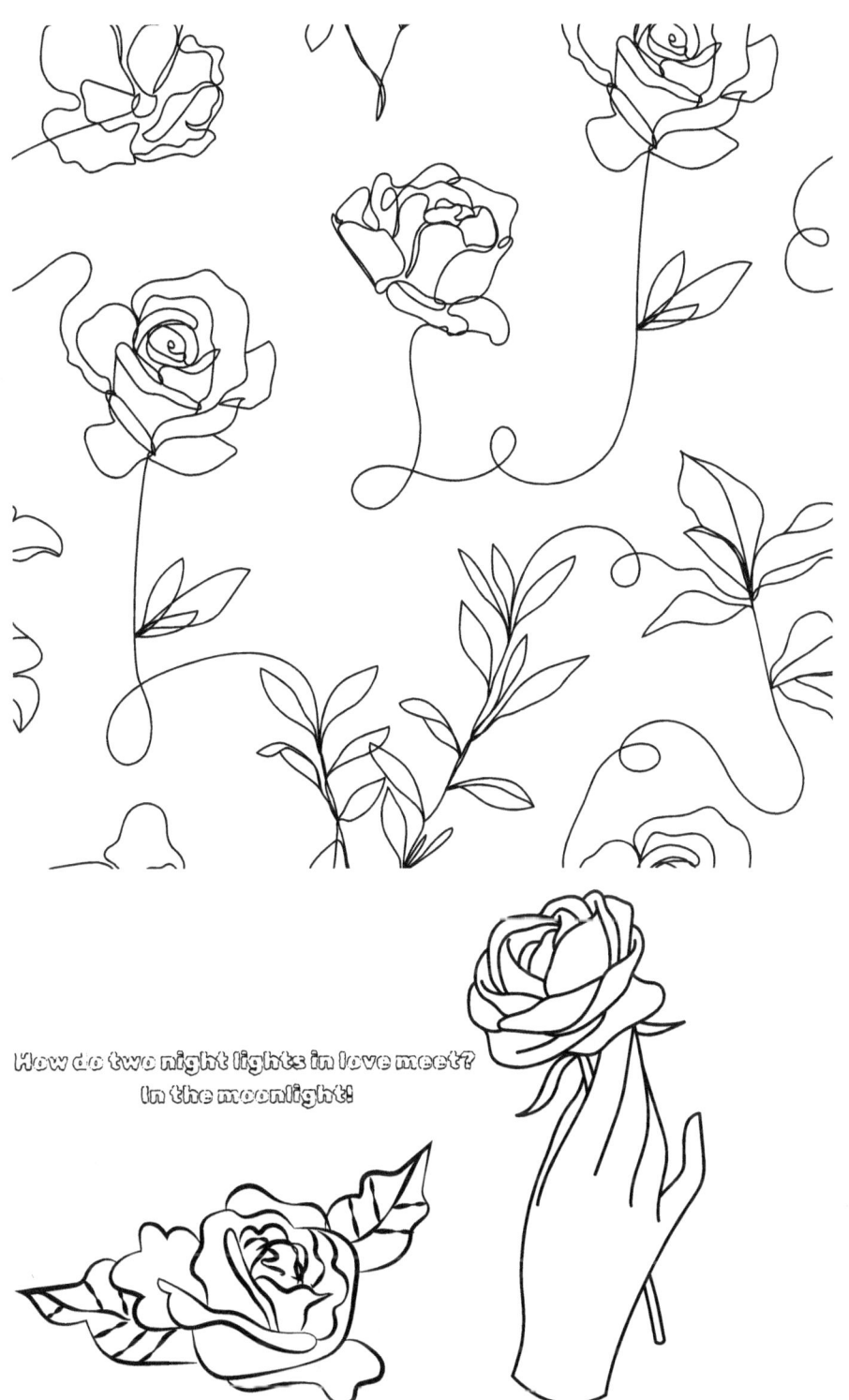

How do two night lights in love meet?
In the moonlight!

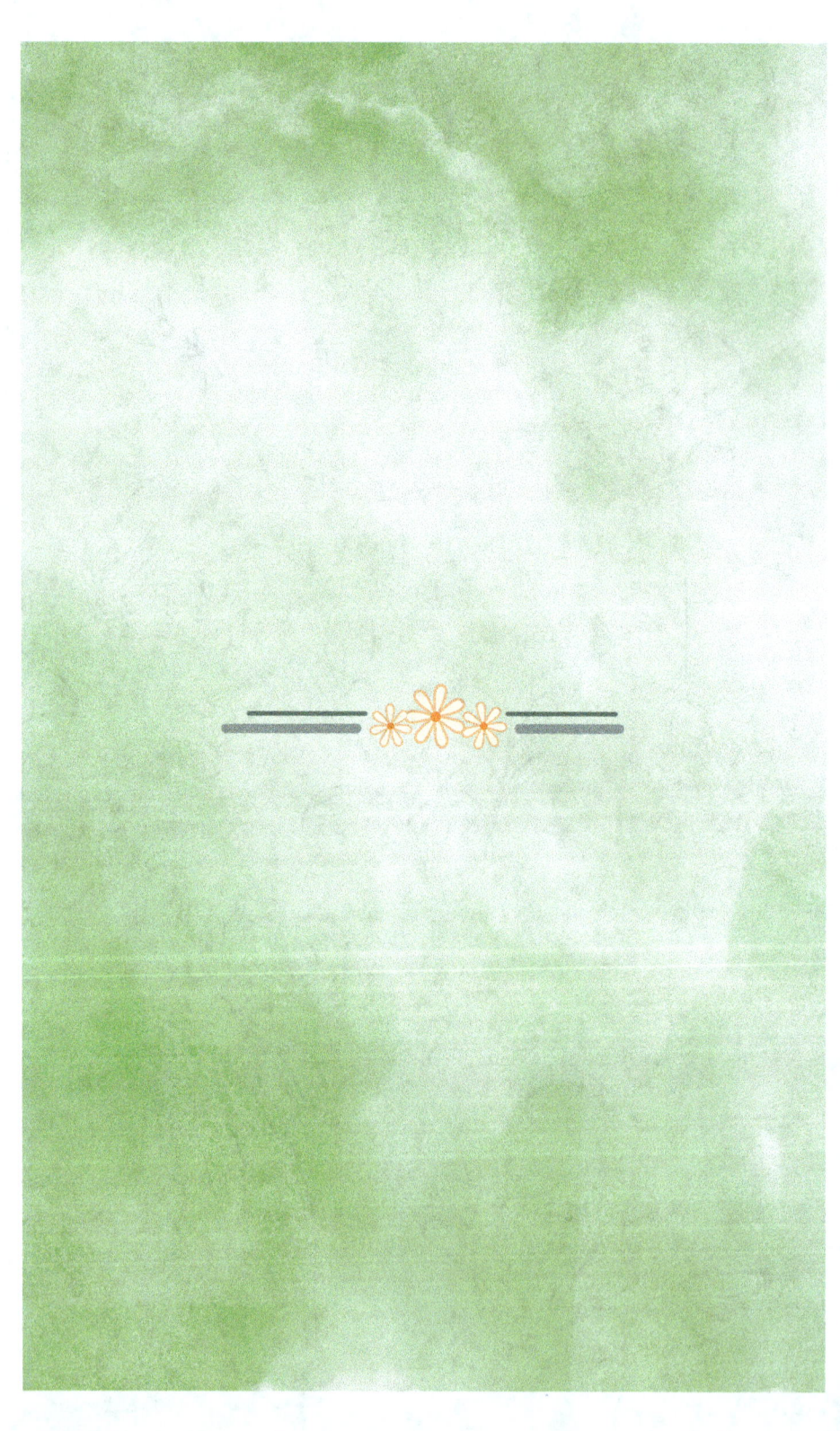

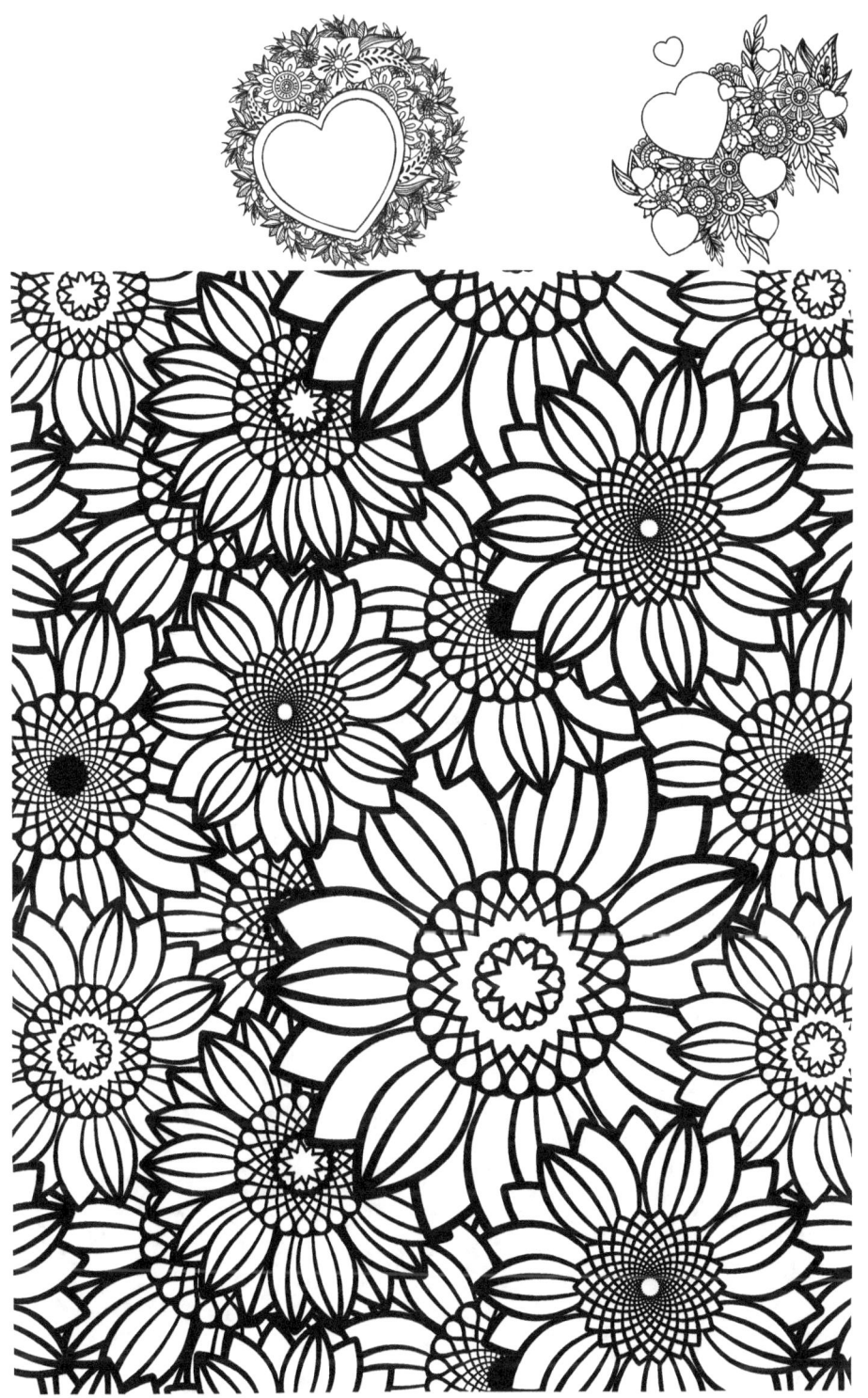

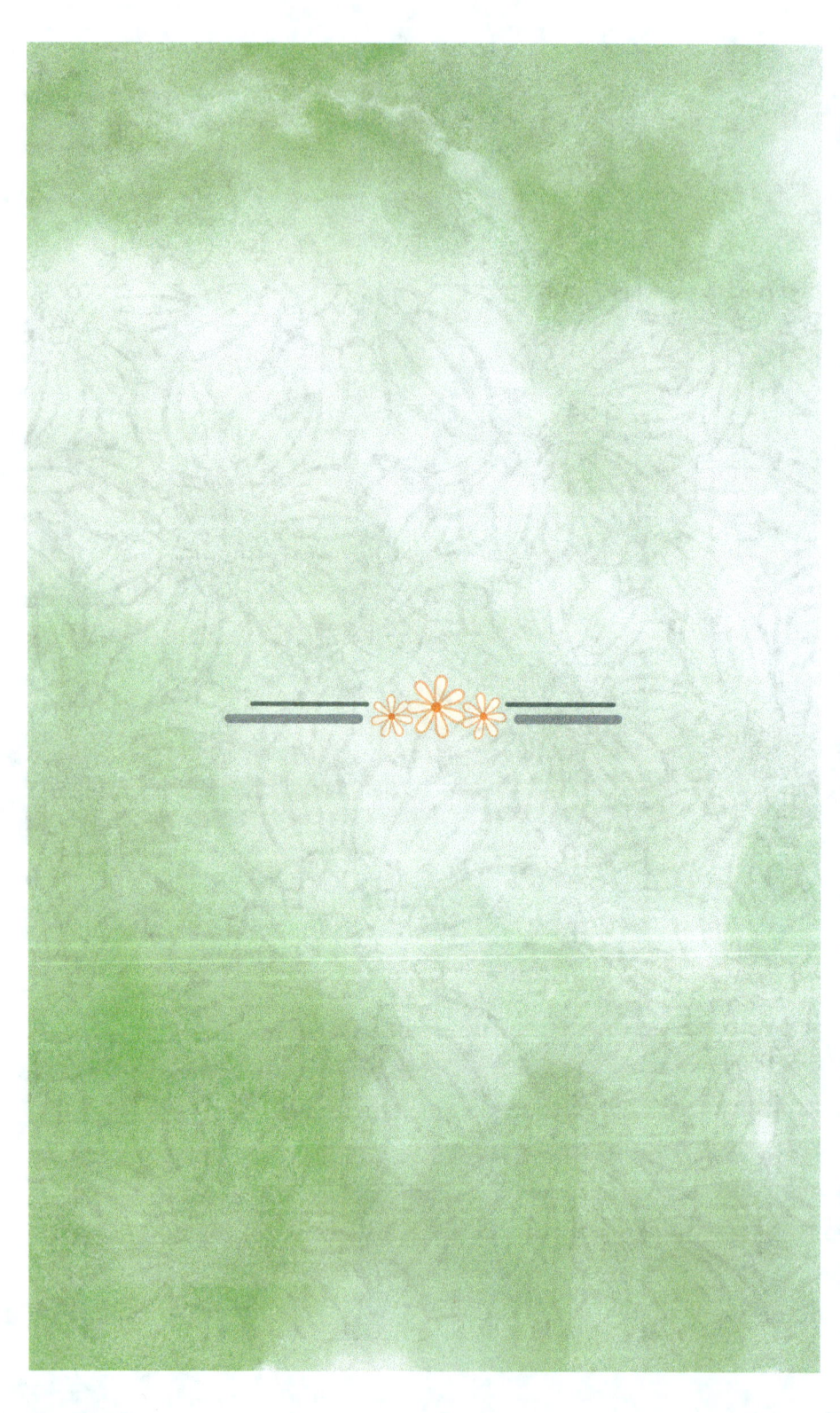

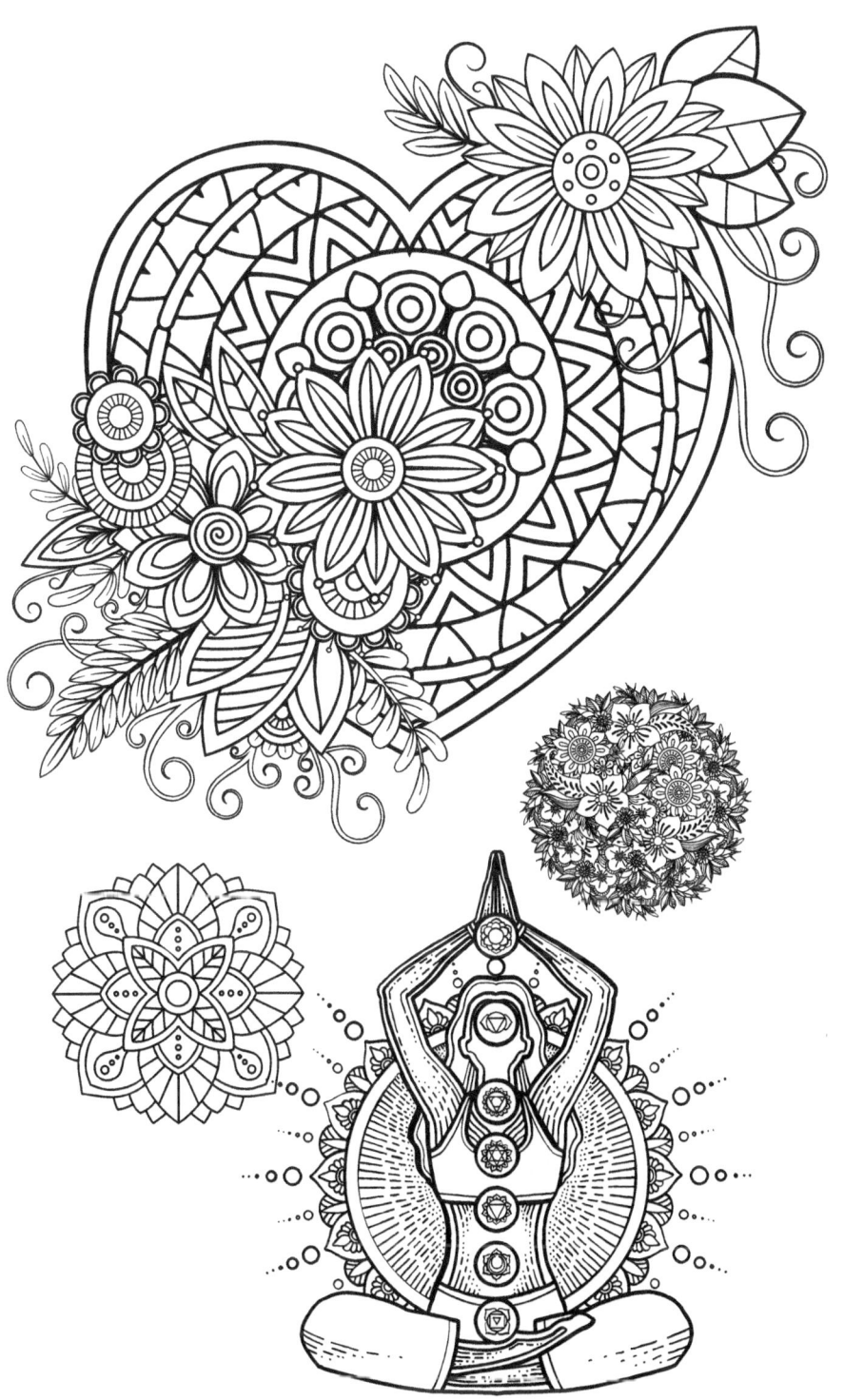

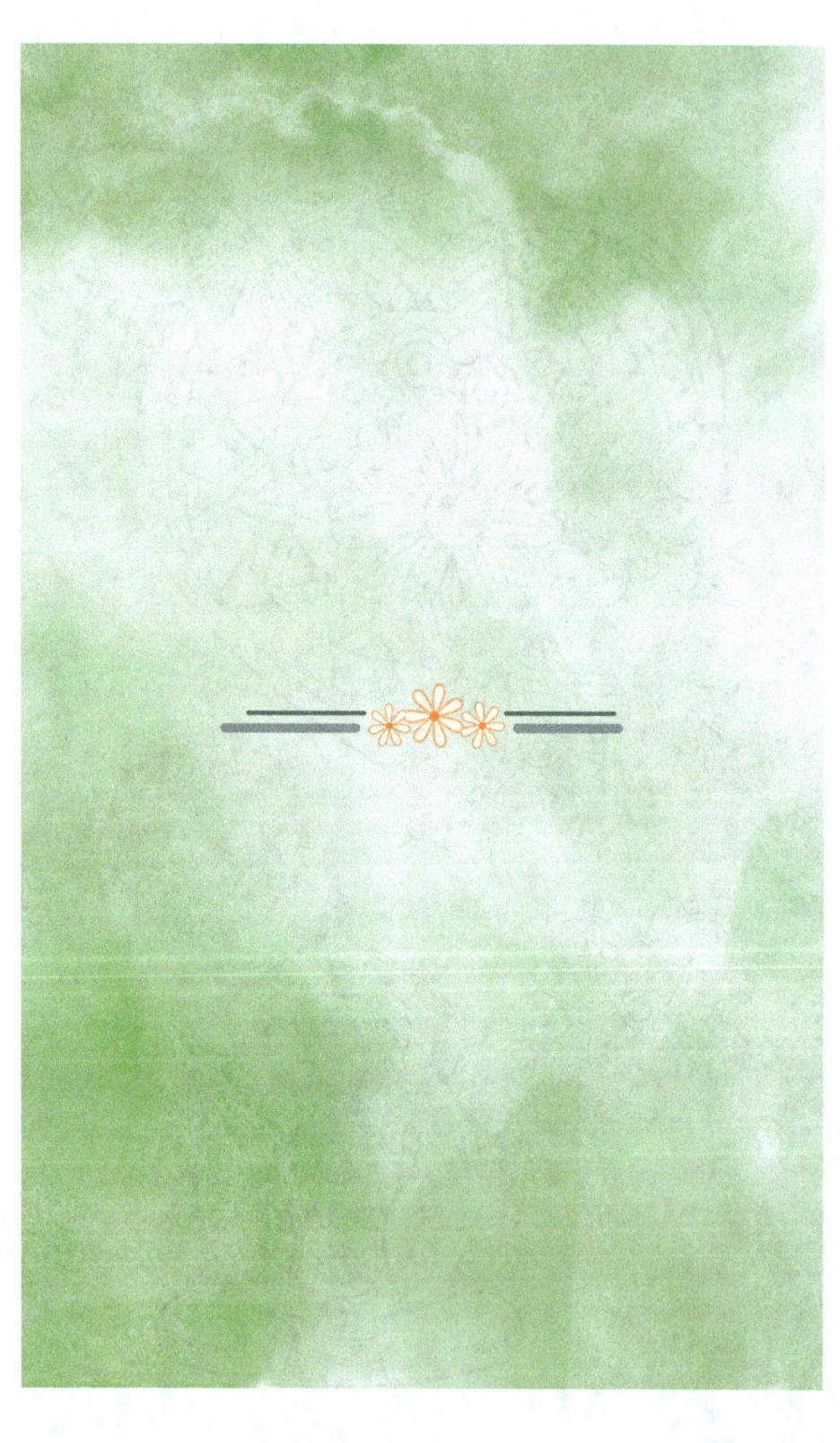

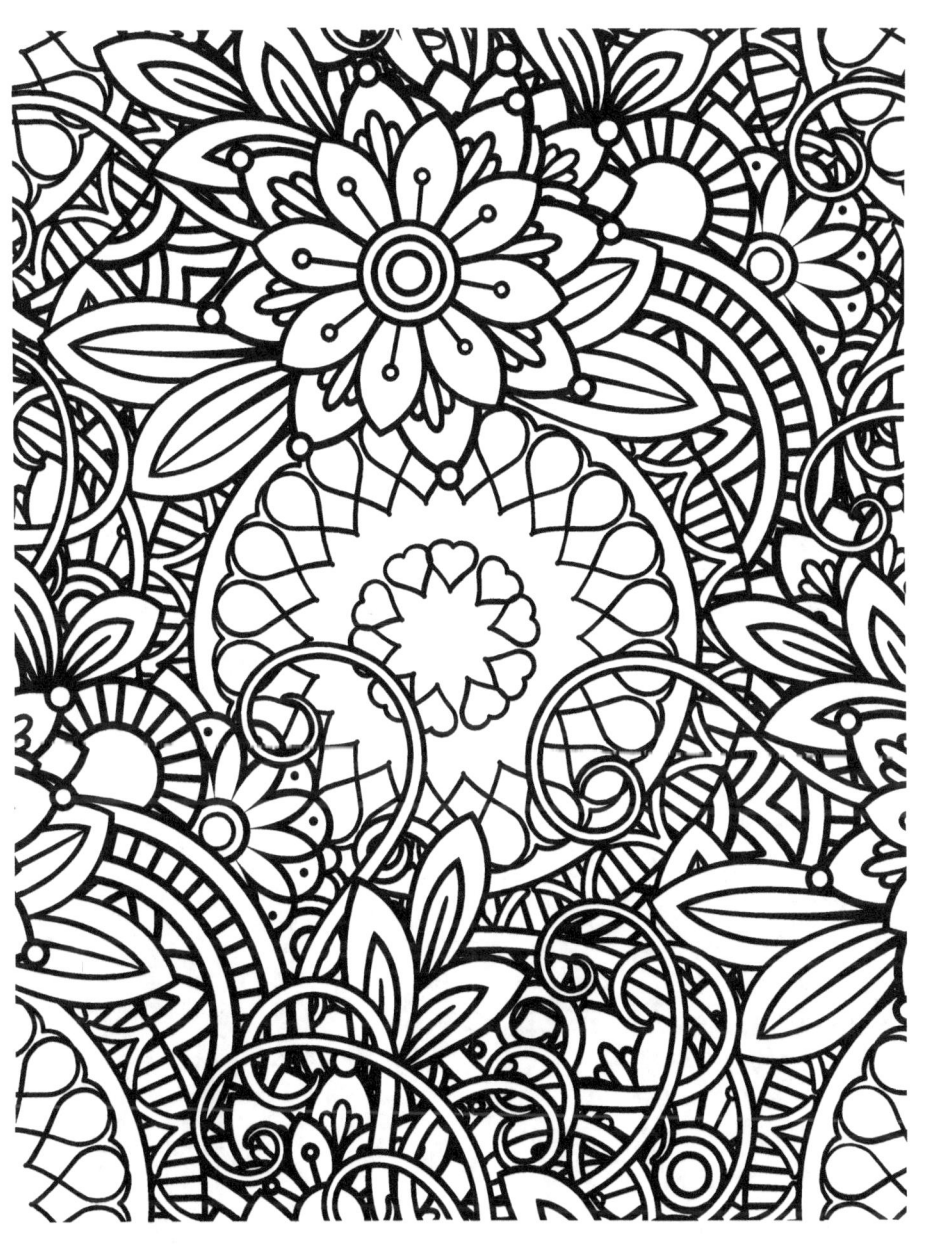

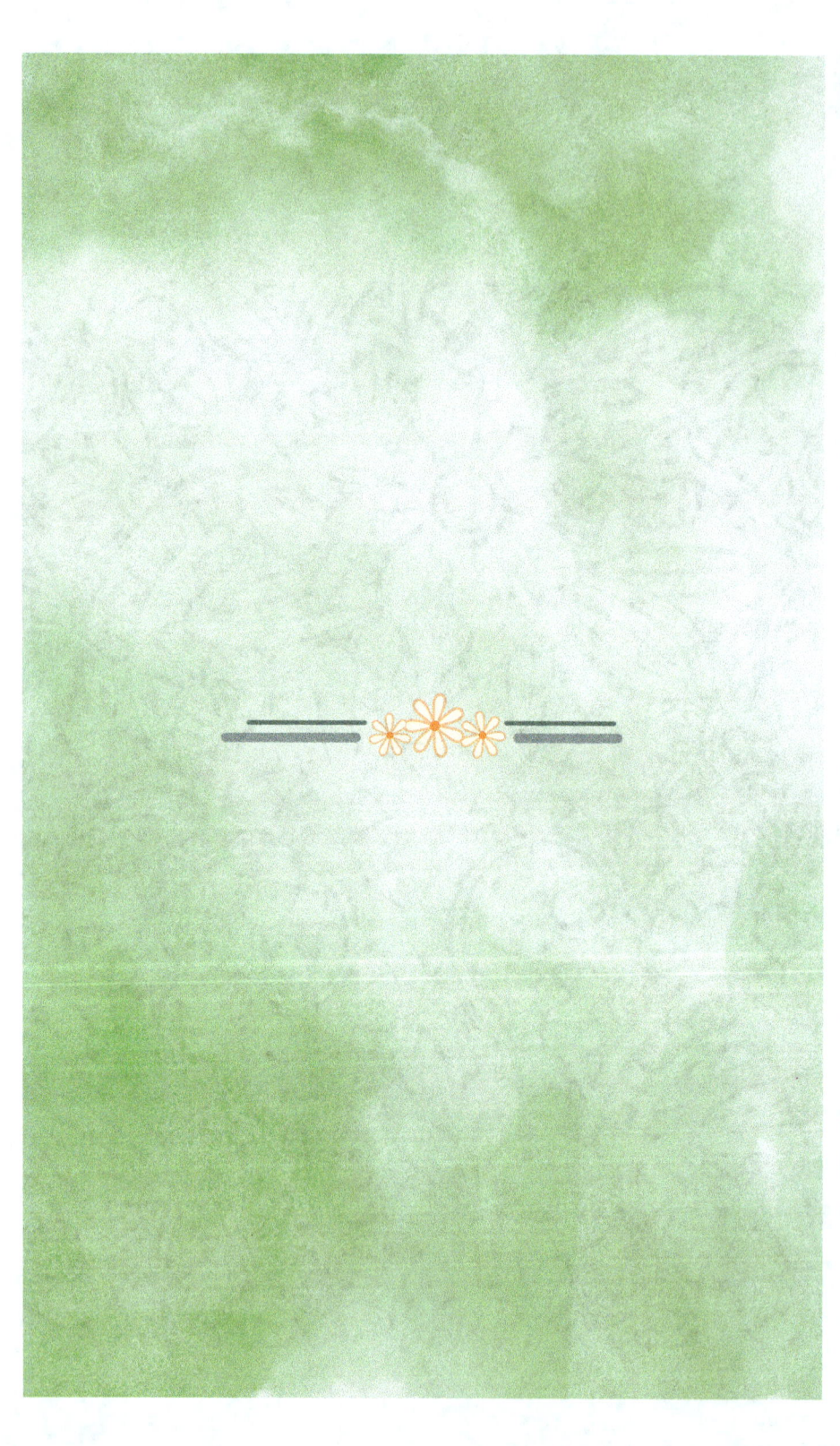

What do you call a husband who never washes the dishes? An expert in "creative culinary arts" with an emphasis on "cooking without dishes"!

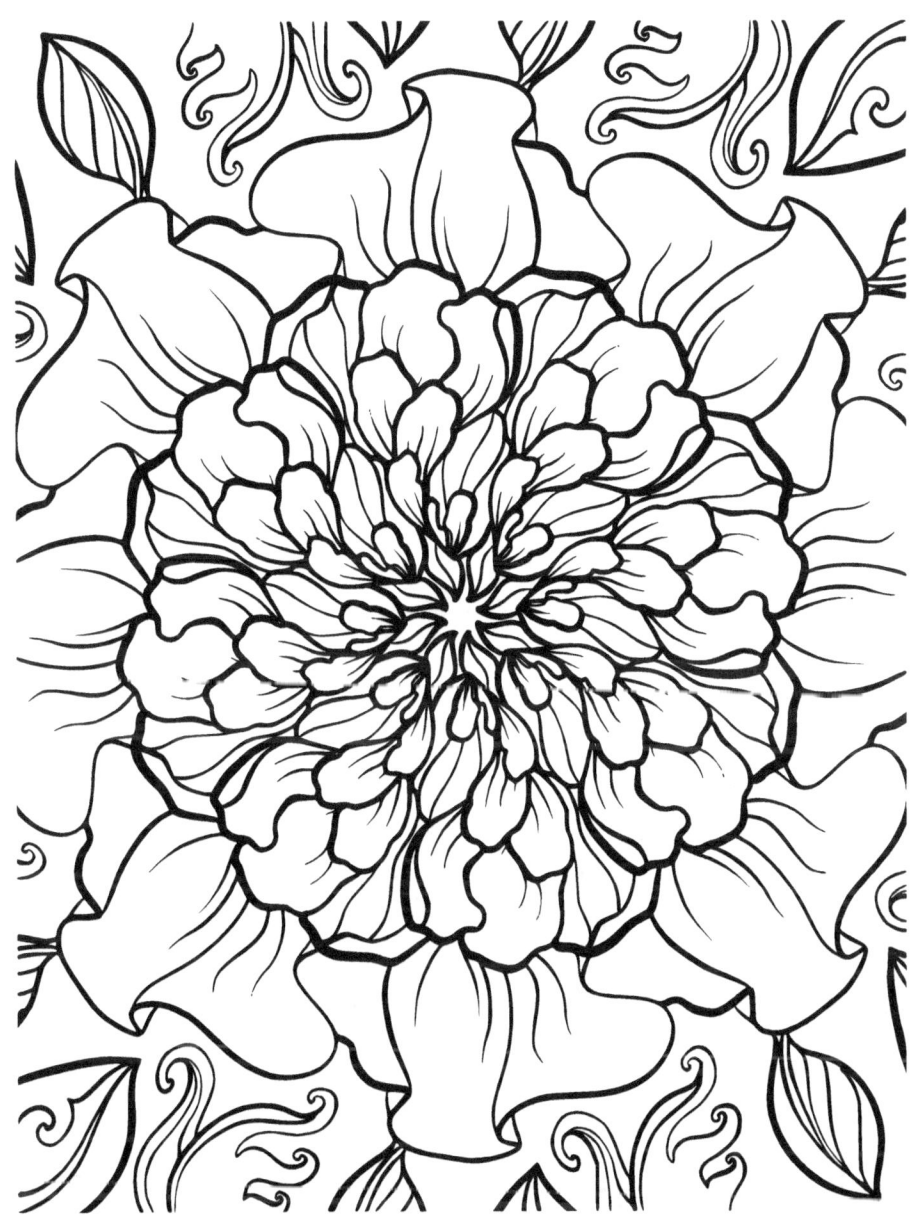

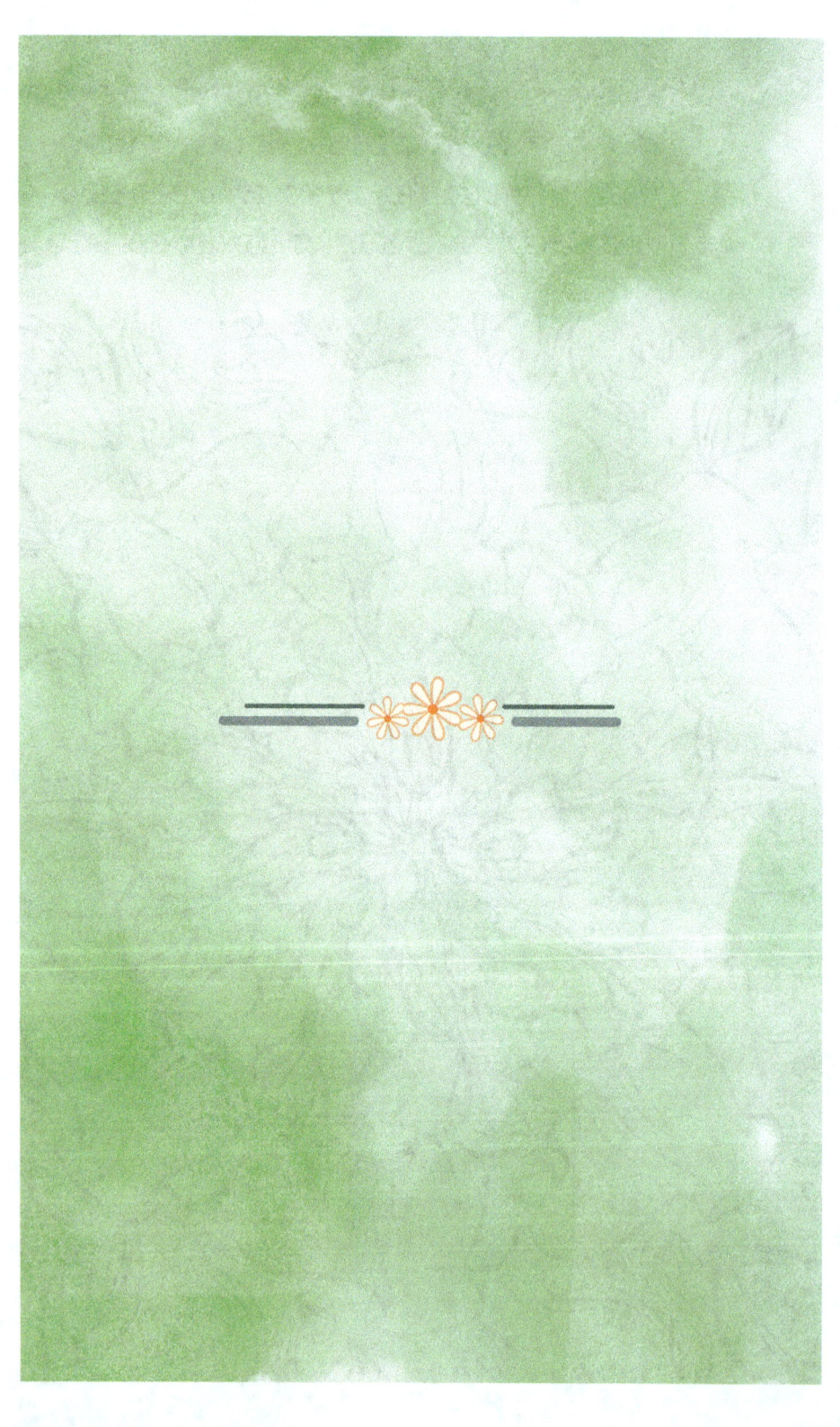

How does Cupid spend his birthday? With a party full of "shooting hearts"!

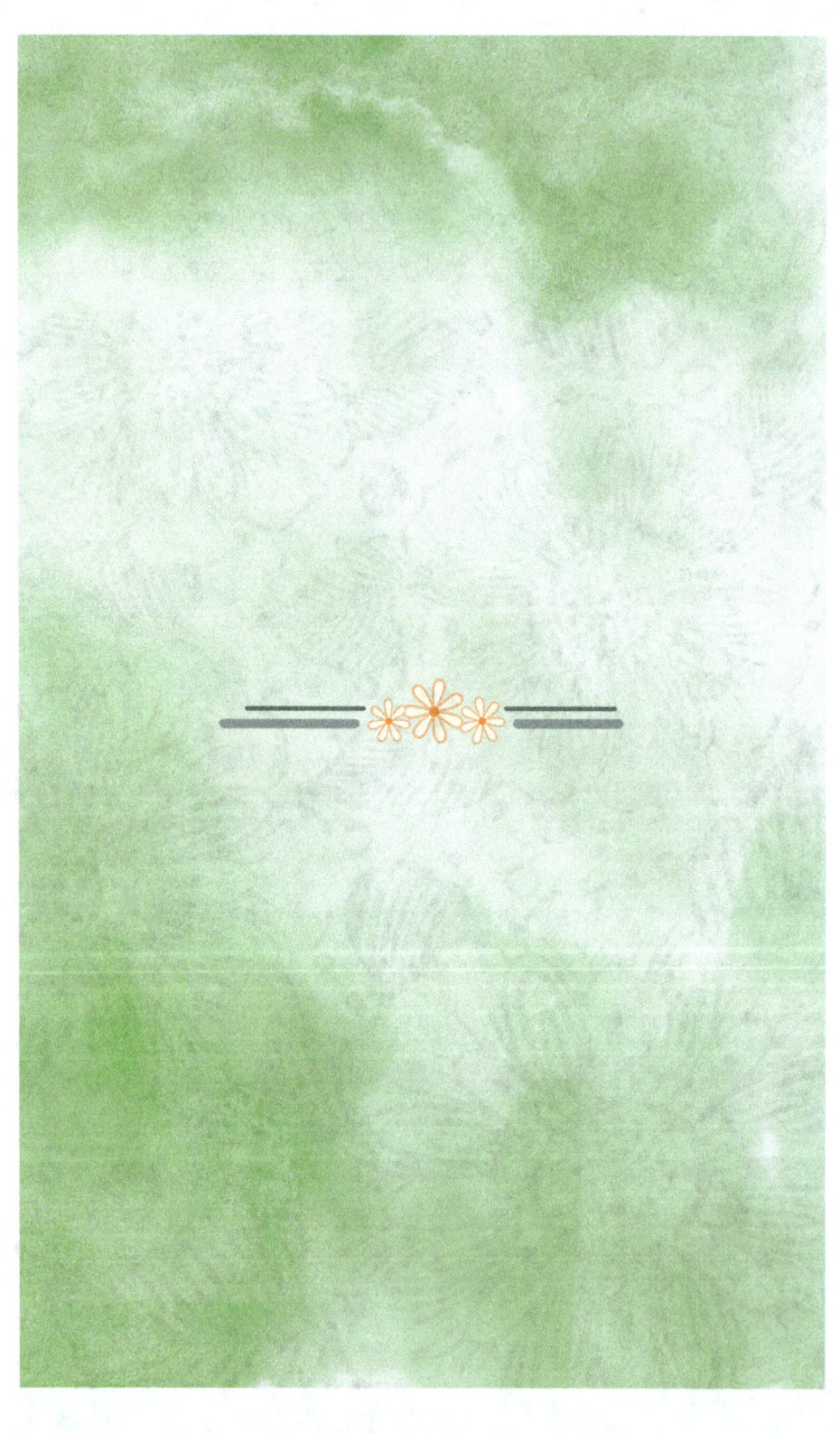

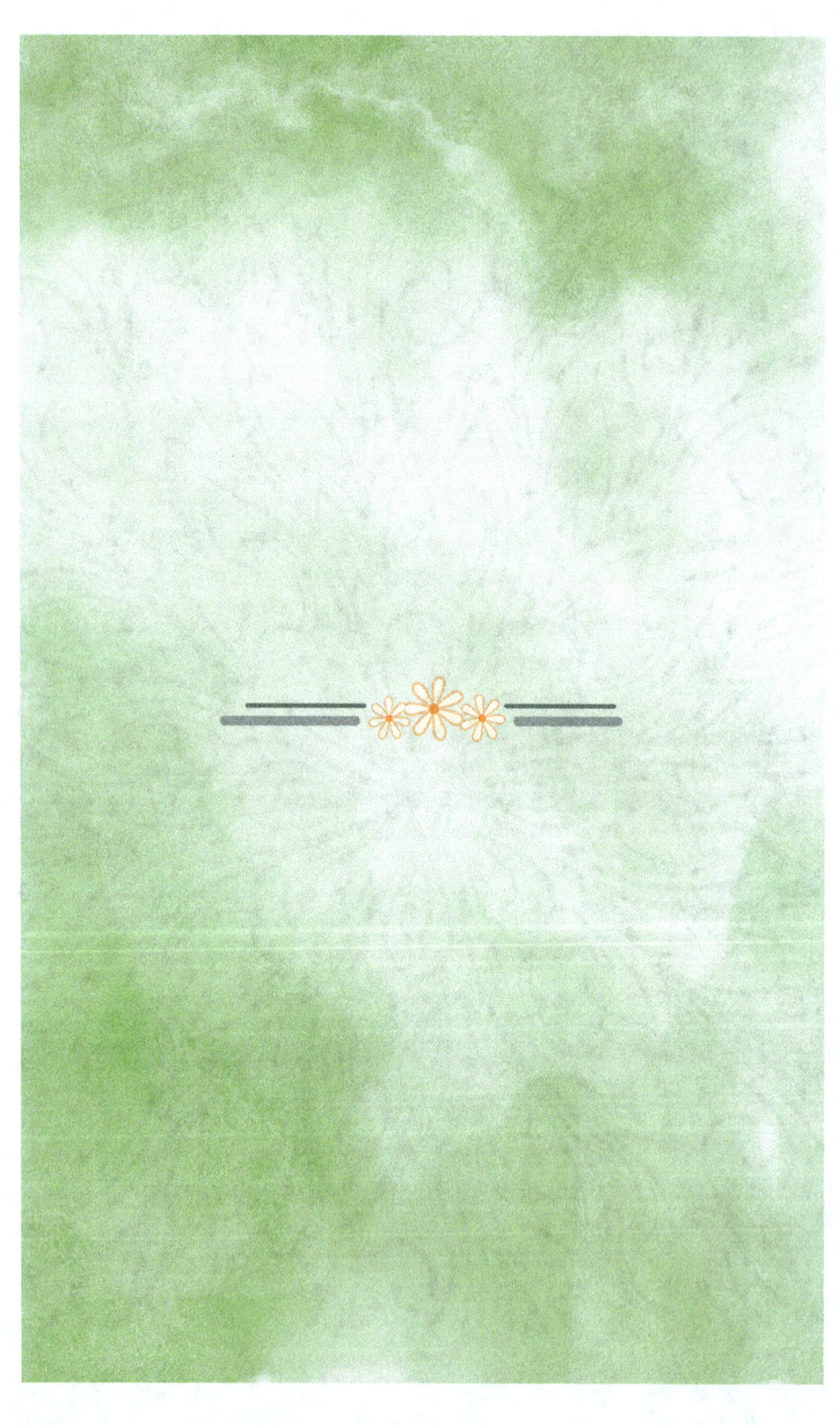

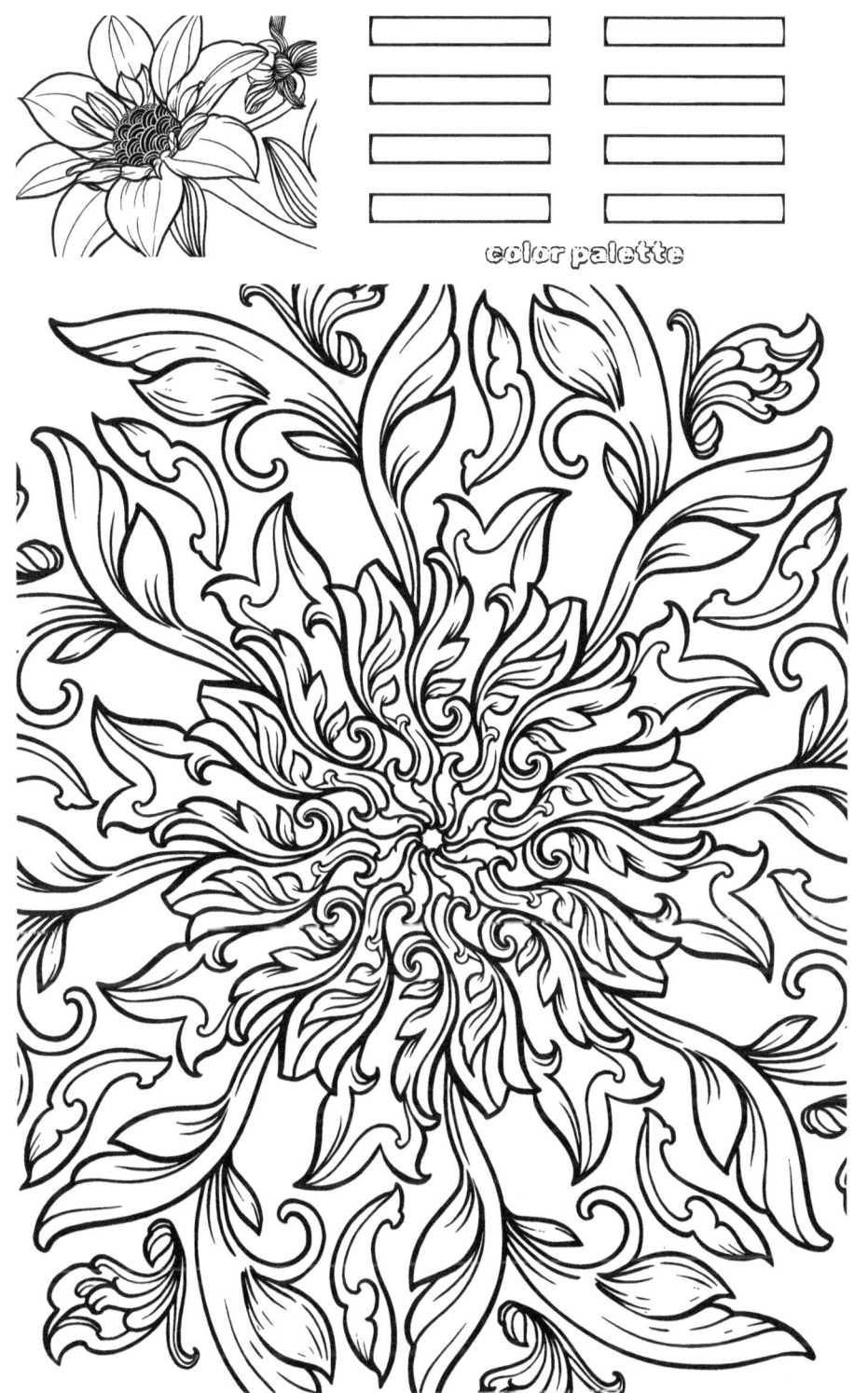

color palette

Why are butterflies so good at dancing?

Because they have "wings" on their feet!

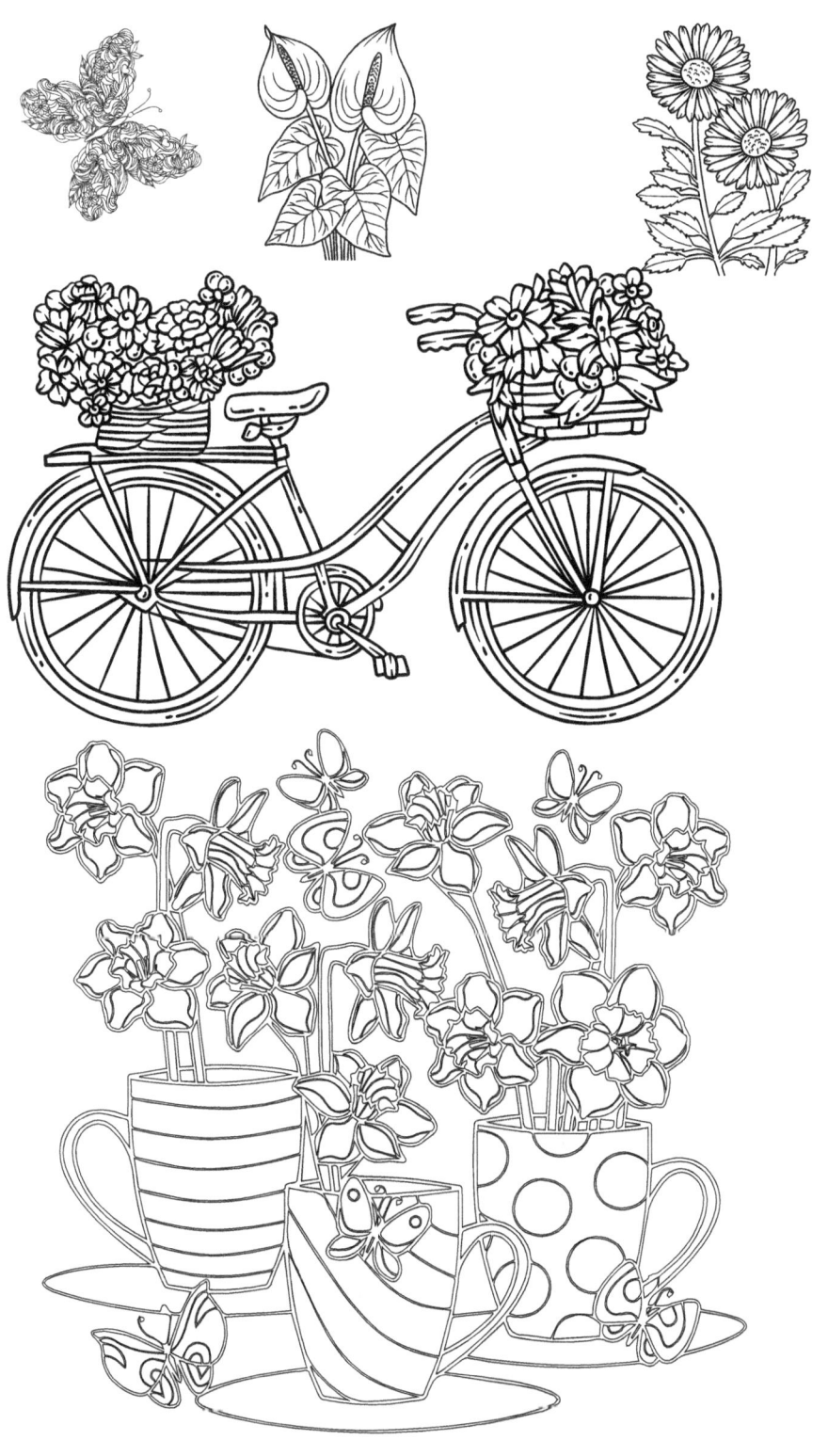

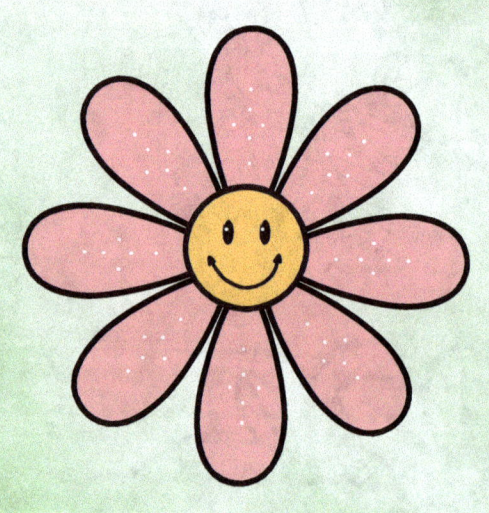

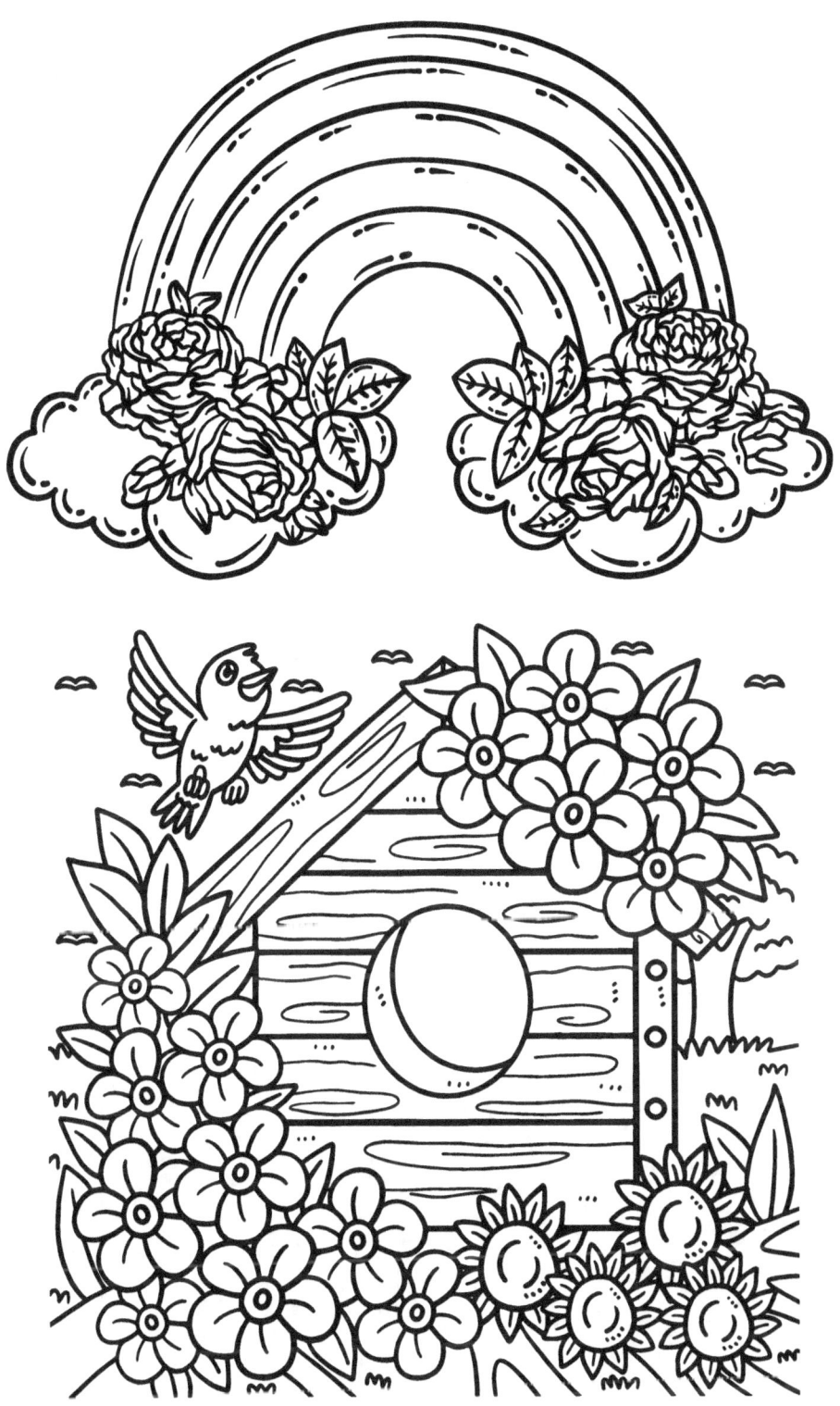

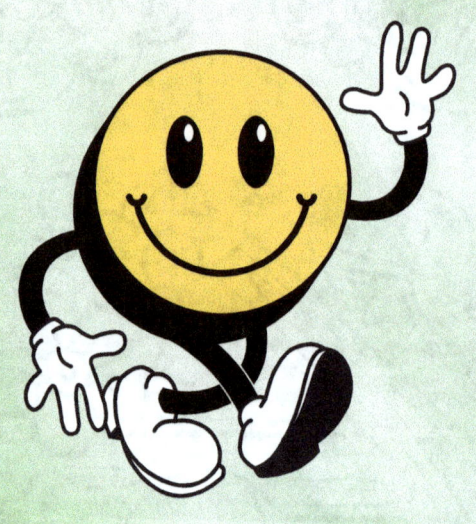

Why did the rose go to the doctor? Because he had a condition called "thorns in the back"!

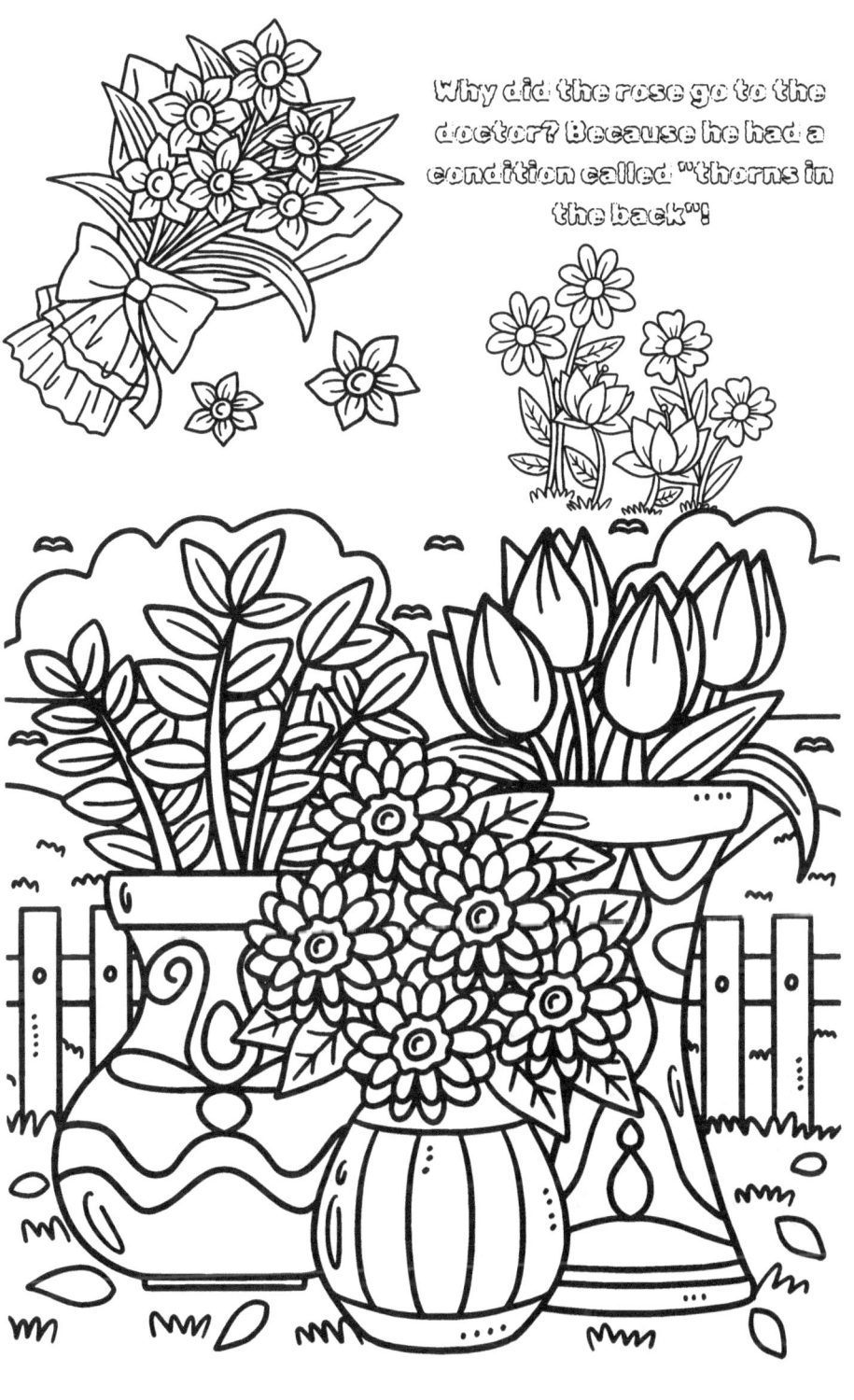

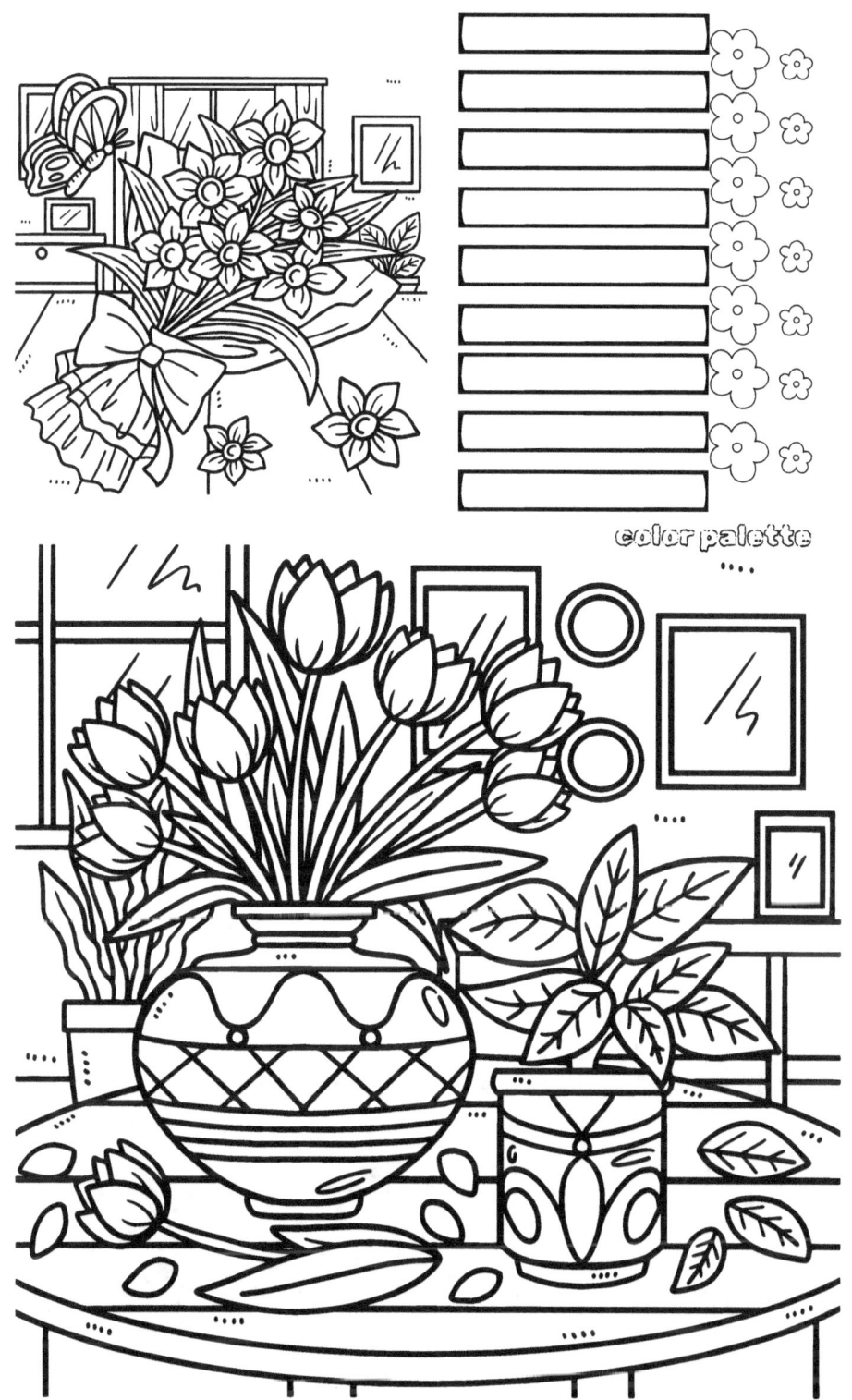

color palette

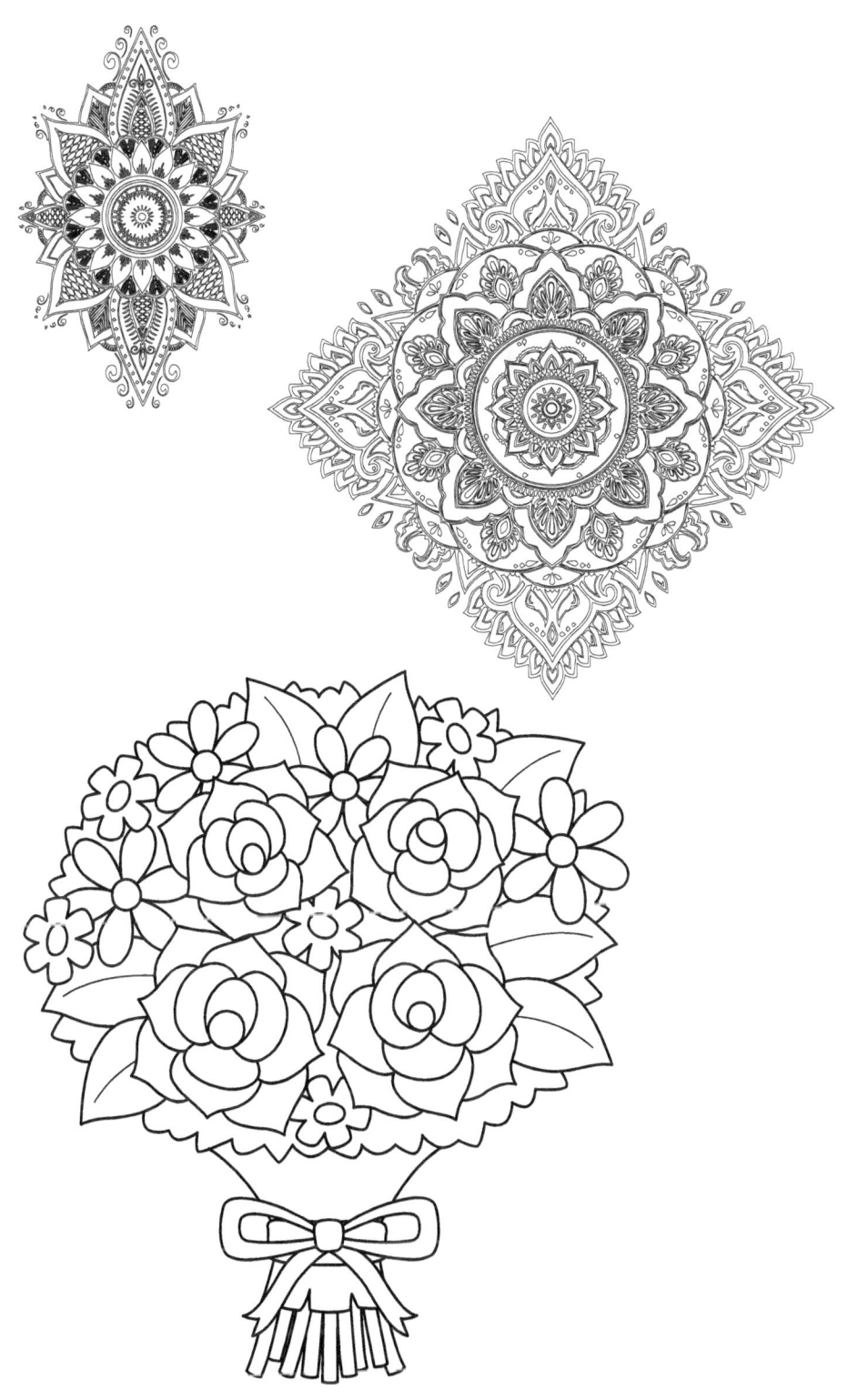

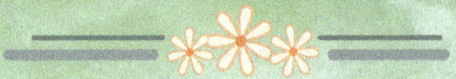

On a beautiful spring day, I saw you and felt that a rare miracle. But you know, my dear, what made me start? That I realized that I didn't put my pants on again!

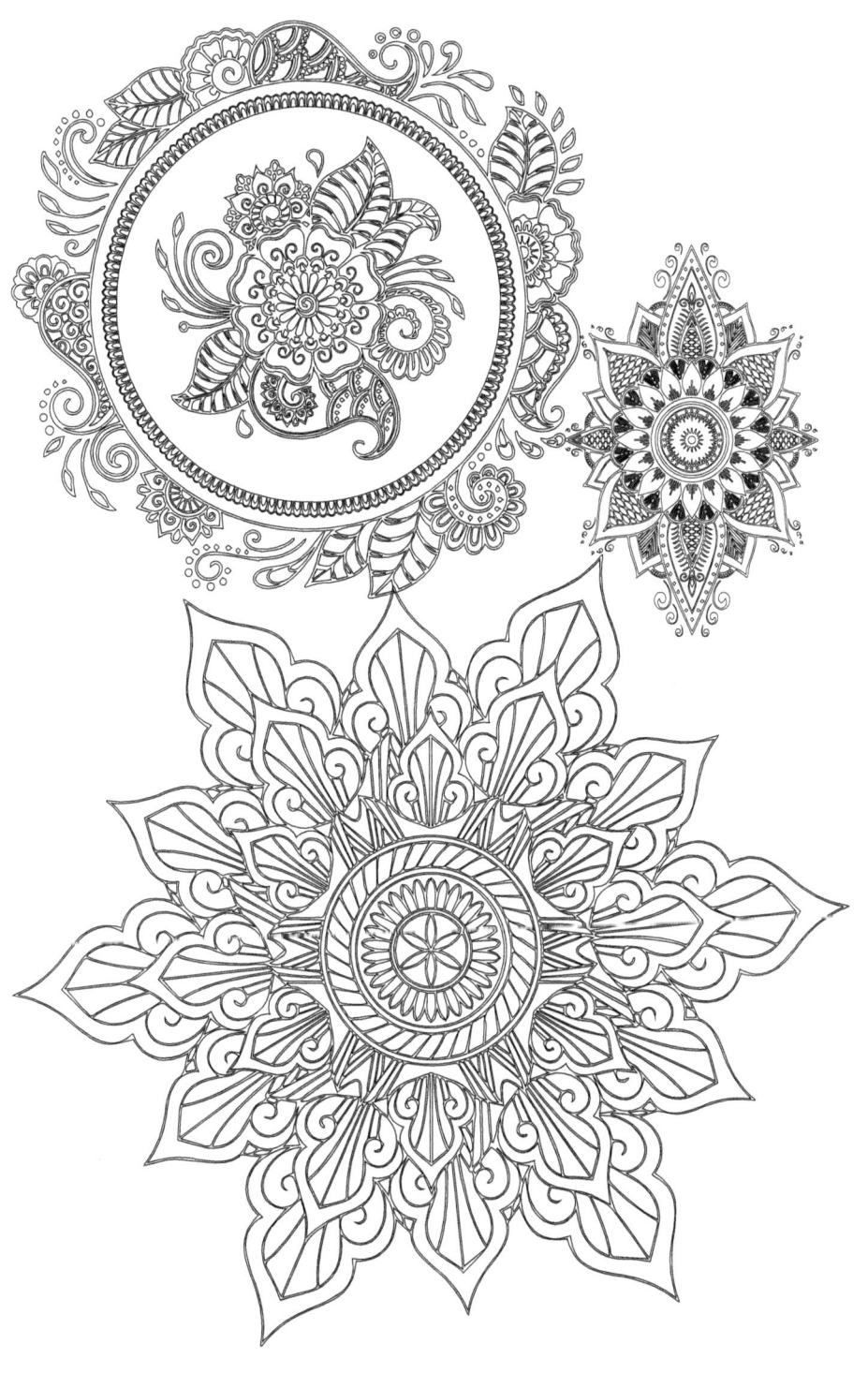

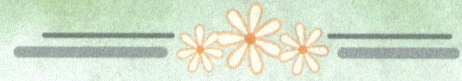

Like a teddy bear I look at you,
In your eyes I lose myself and melt.
But you must know, my beloved wife,
When you're snoring like a tractor at night, you're not so stylish!

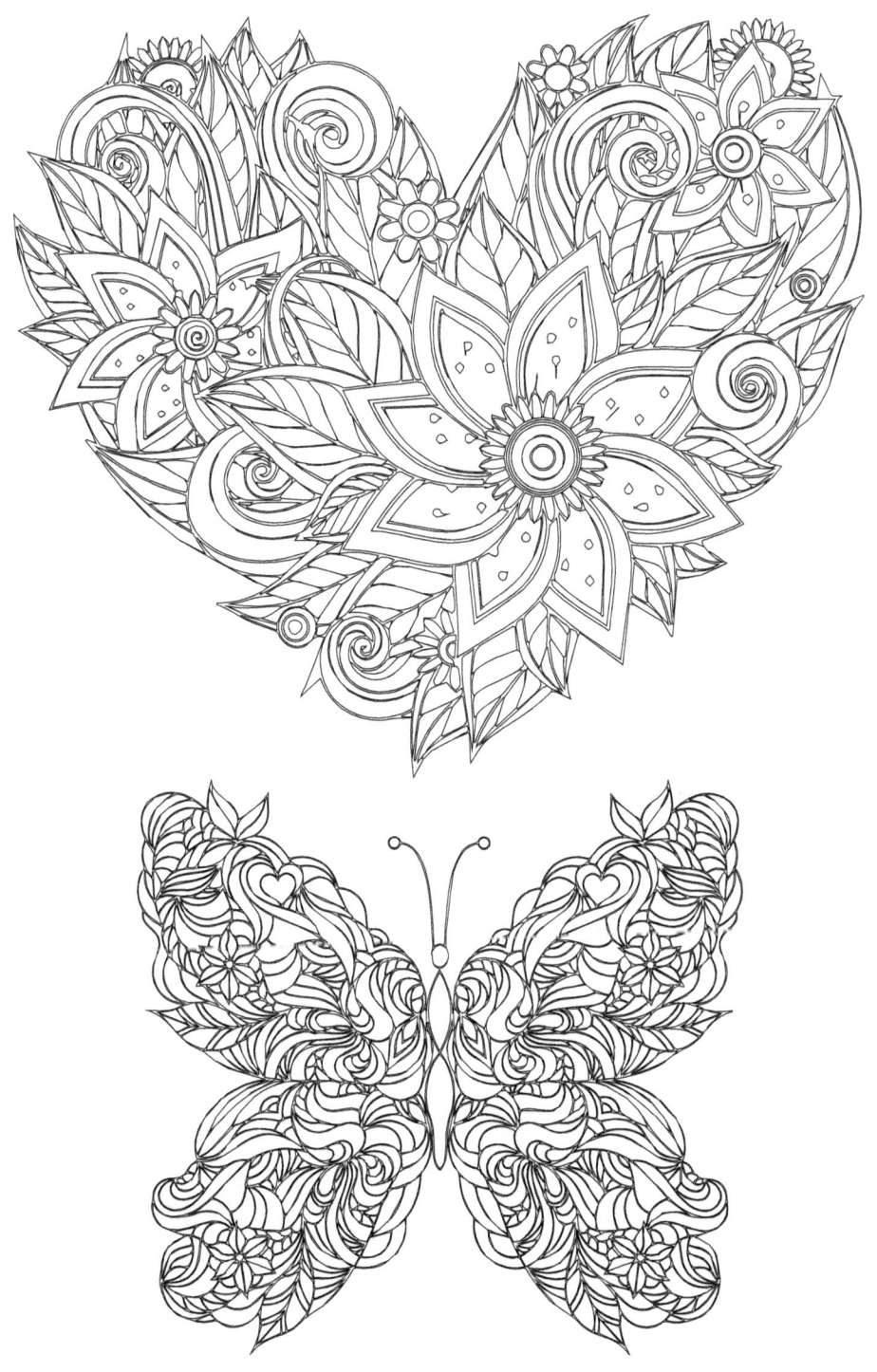

In the universe of my heart, you are the star,
Without you, life would just be a bitter joke.
But know, my boundless love,
You better do something about your sleepwalking, because at night you're dancing around the house like a garden elf!

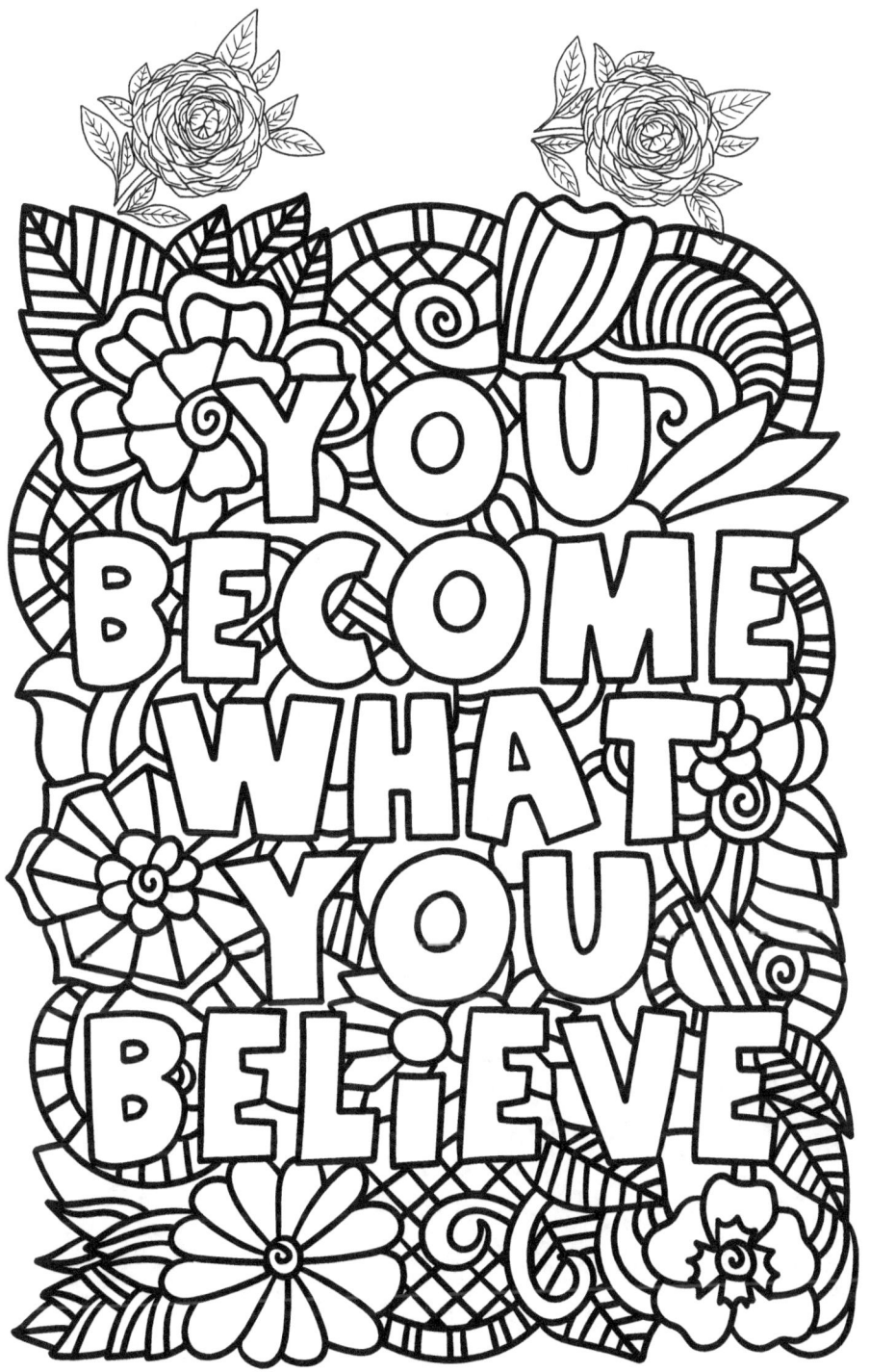

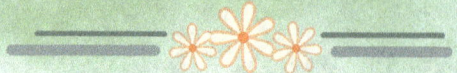

My cold thought whispers,
Because I would be lost in the night.
And in the shining darkness,
I put the light aside.
I'm no longer looking for the peak of life,
And neither is the clay from the deep.
Nor the morning light,
I don't want to touch her anymore.
For playing with broken strings.
Here it no longer amazes me,
Even as the sun goes down
Nor how the moon in the lake looks.
And if I were to keep my path,
And in the fog to sleep.
I loved you like the wind loves the sea,
Like the waves of the ocean break me from the
shore
The thought of our love remains in my mind
And I kiss you gently and warmly
dear mother

Why are the trees never lost in the forest? Because they always have orientation leaves!

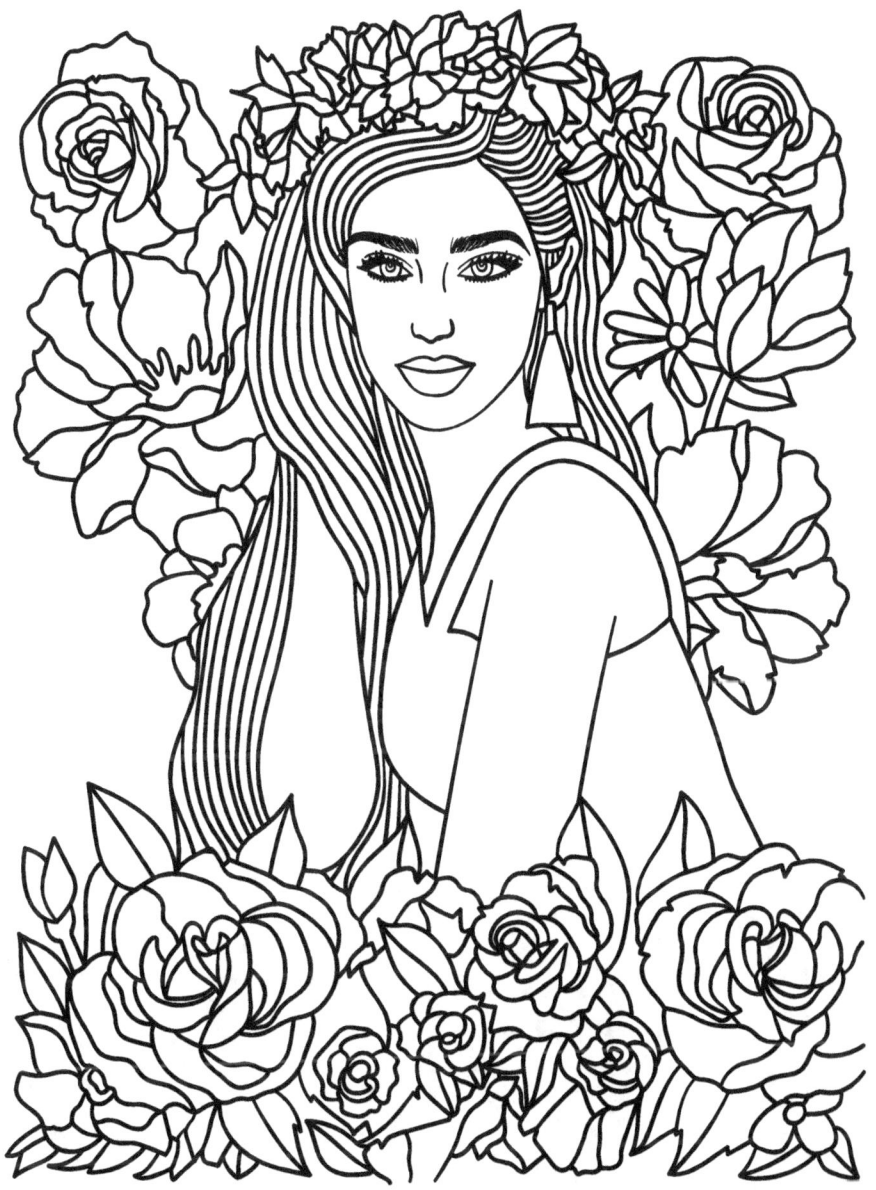

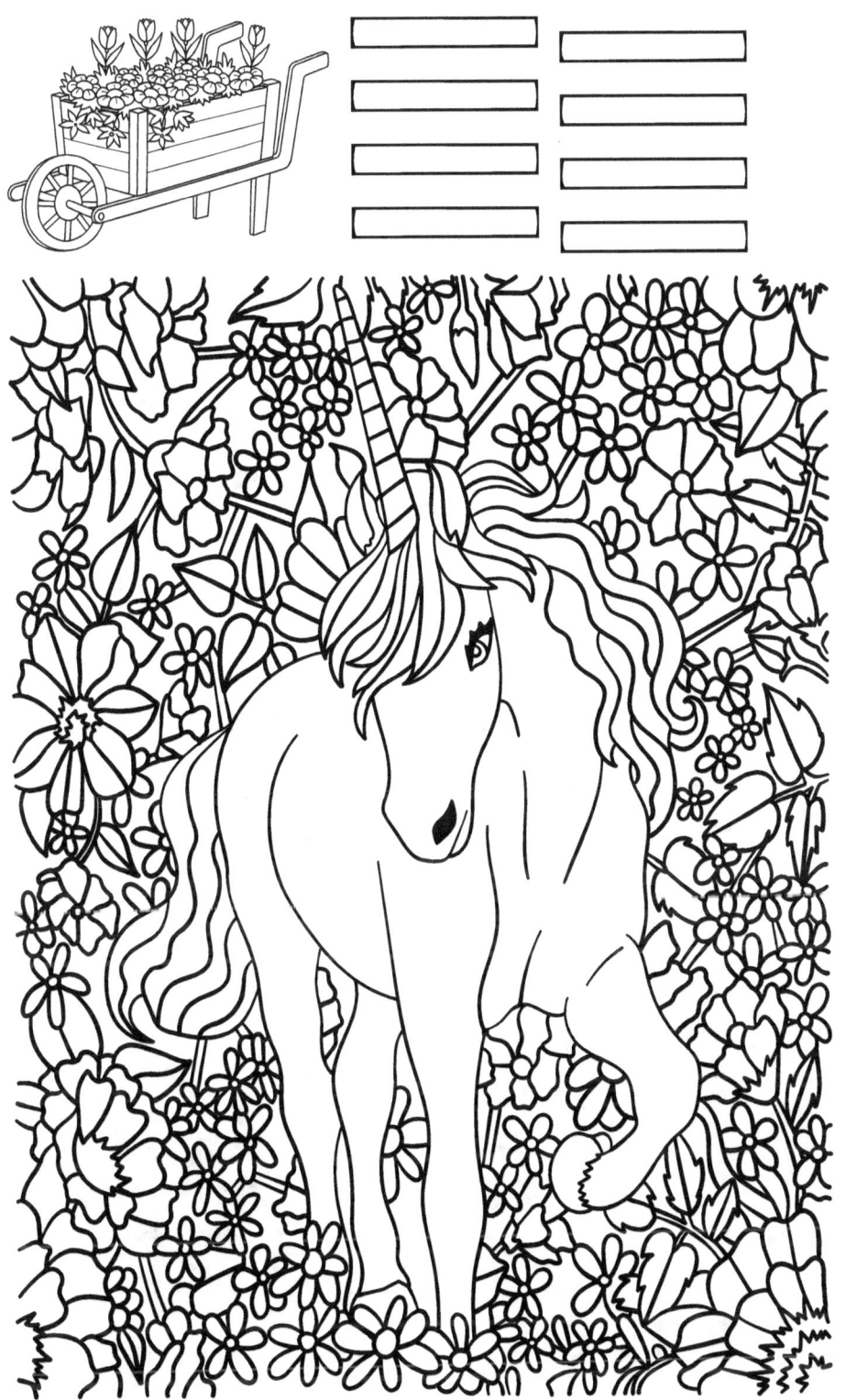

I hunted close, I hunted far
I even looked inside my car.
I lost my glasses, I need
Let me have them now so I can
read them.
I swear out loud and swear
Did I leave them in my purse?
Are they behind the sofa, under
the bed?
Oh, there it is—on my head!

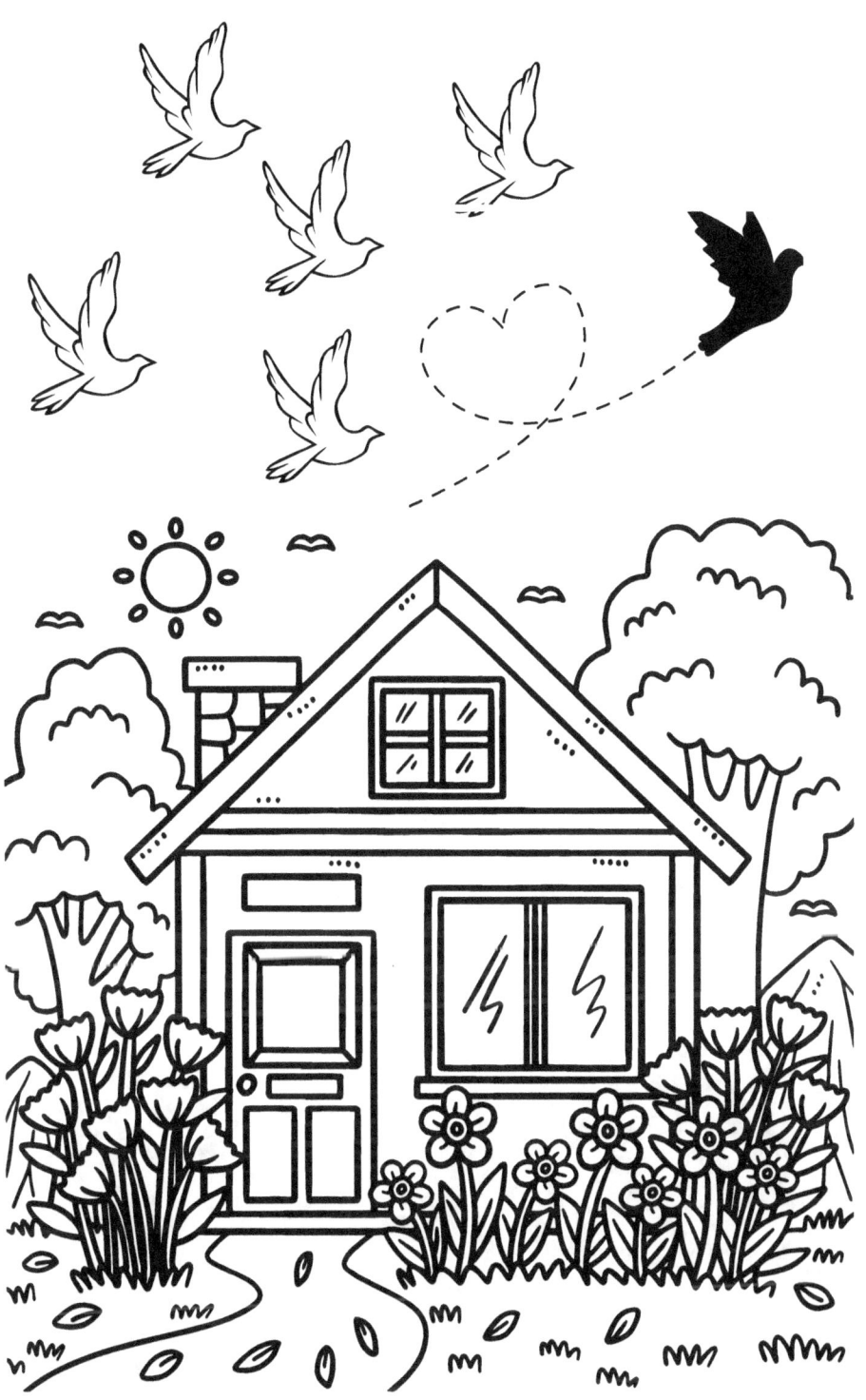

What is the difference between wife and detective mysteries? While police mysteries always have a solution, the wife can be a mystery even after years of marriage!

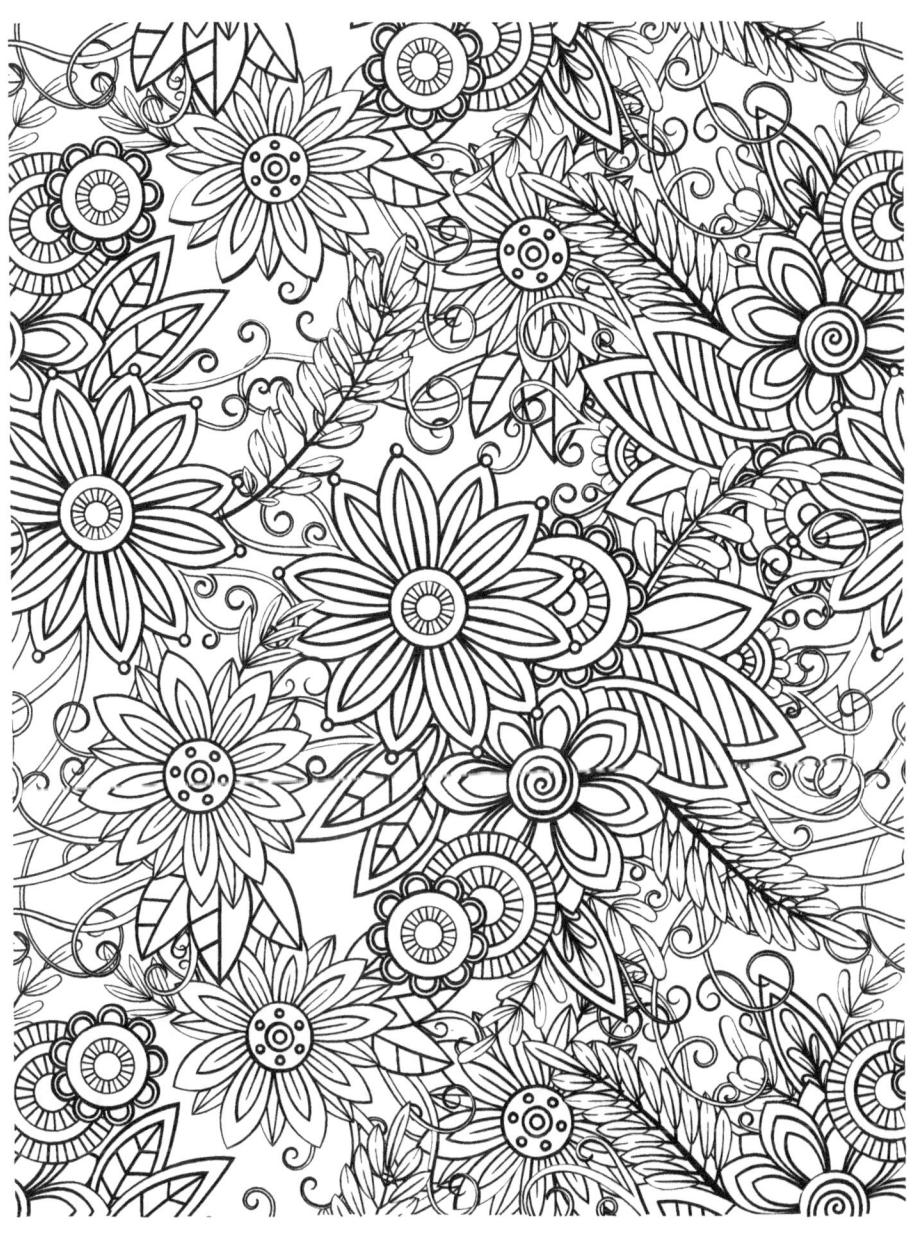

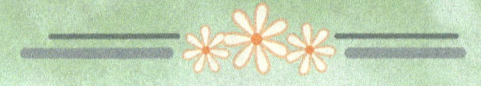

The weather comes, the weather passes
Like water from the spring.
Back she doesn't come back
As long as you don't die

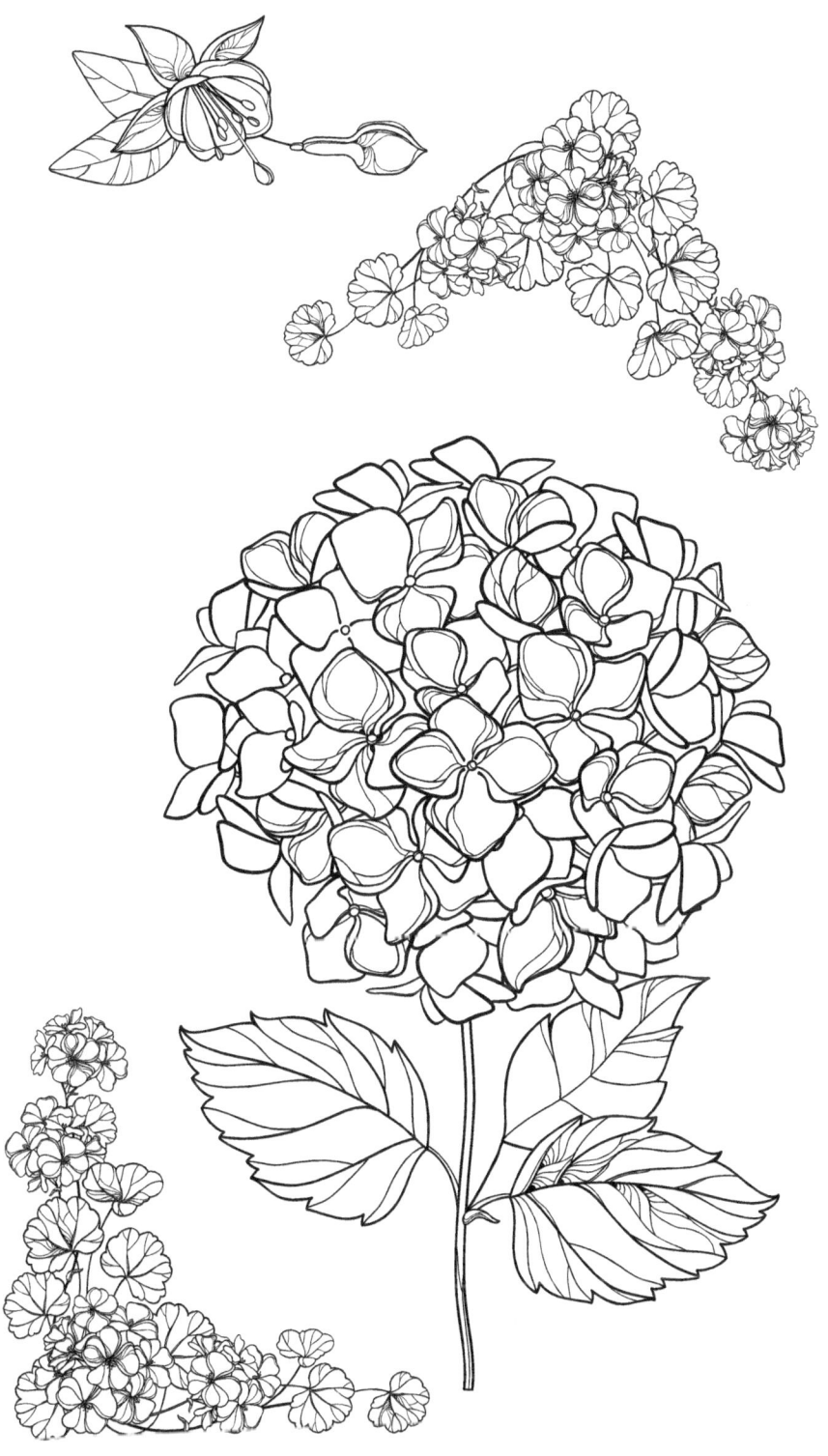

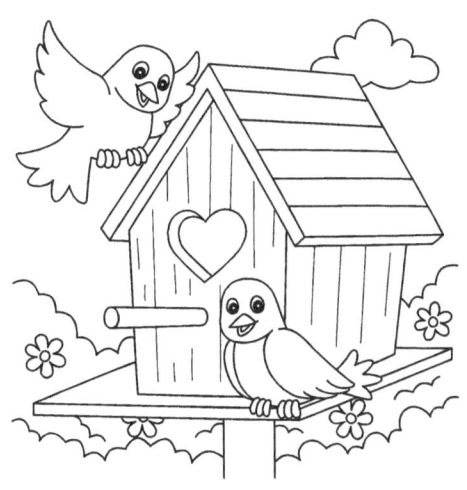

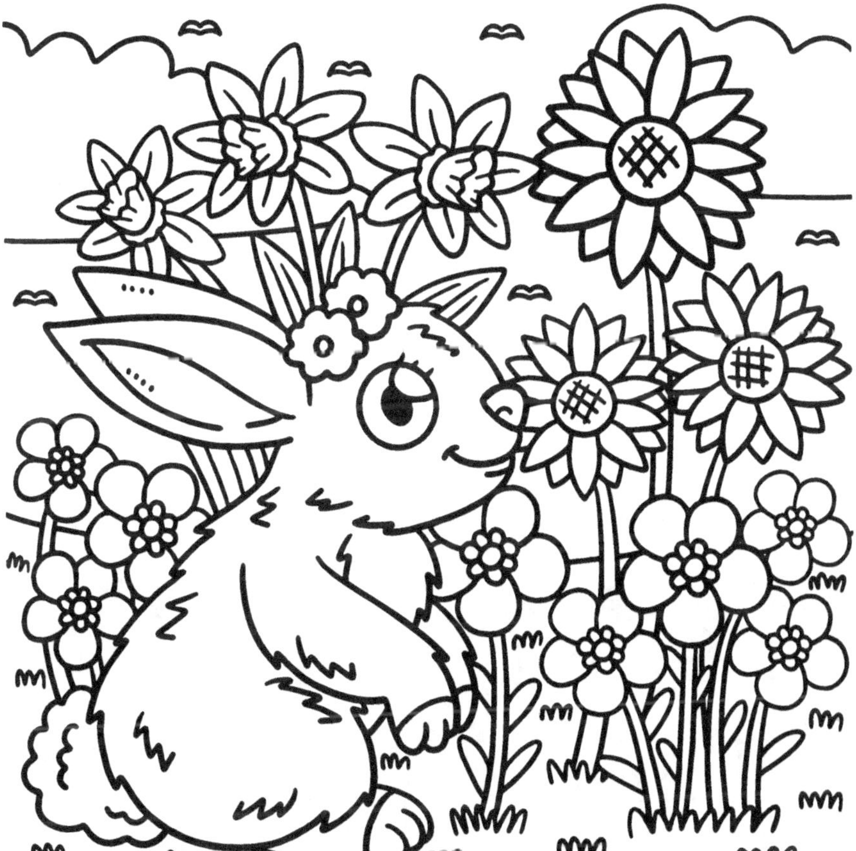

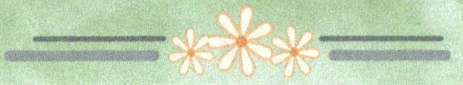

What does a chicken do when it laughs? It's making eggs!

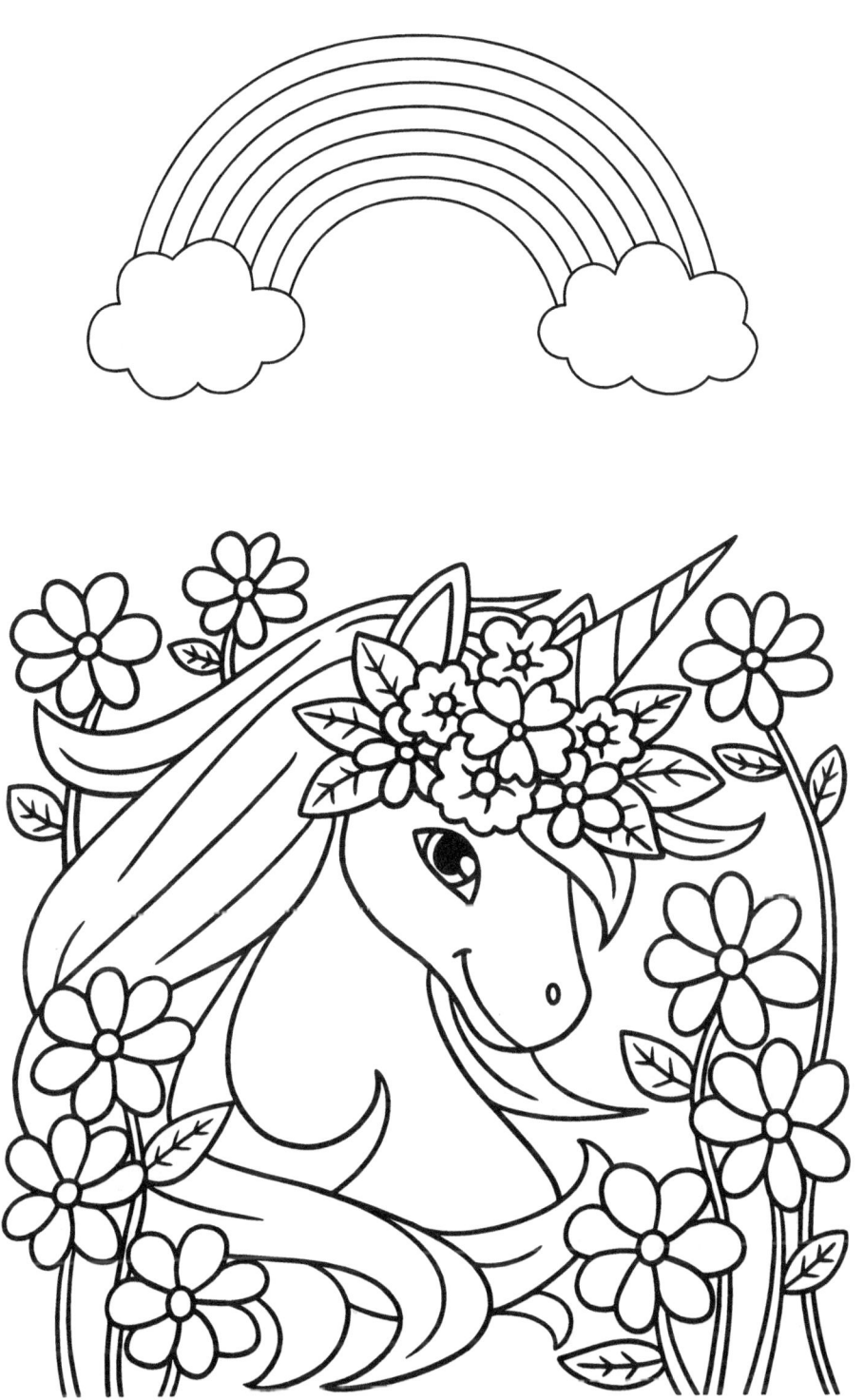

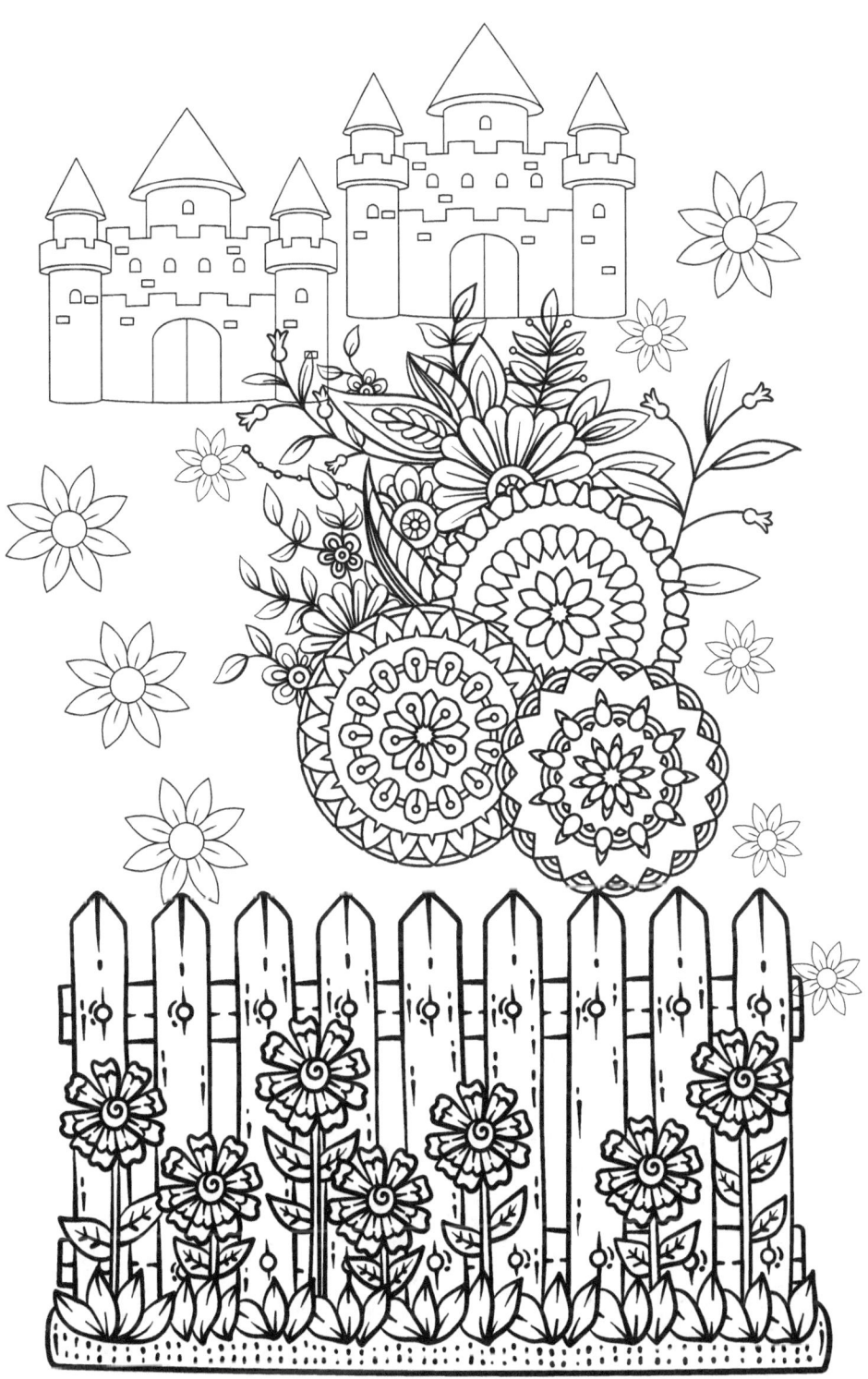

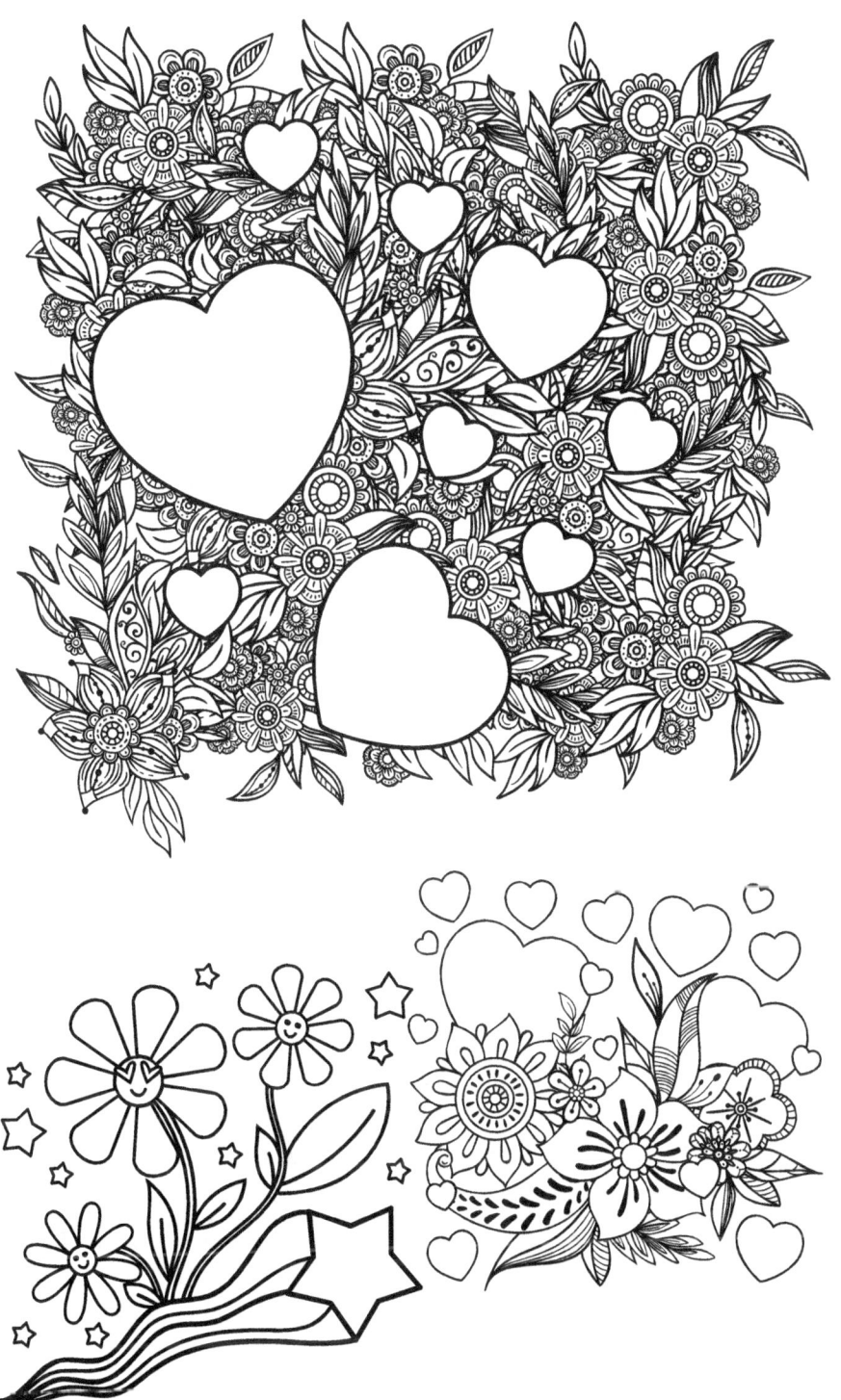

How do two flowers spend time together? Through romantic "flowerings"!

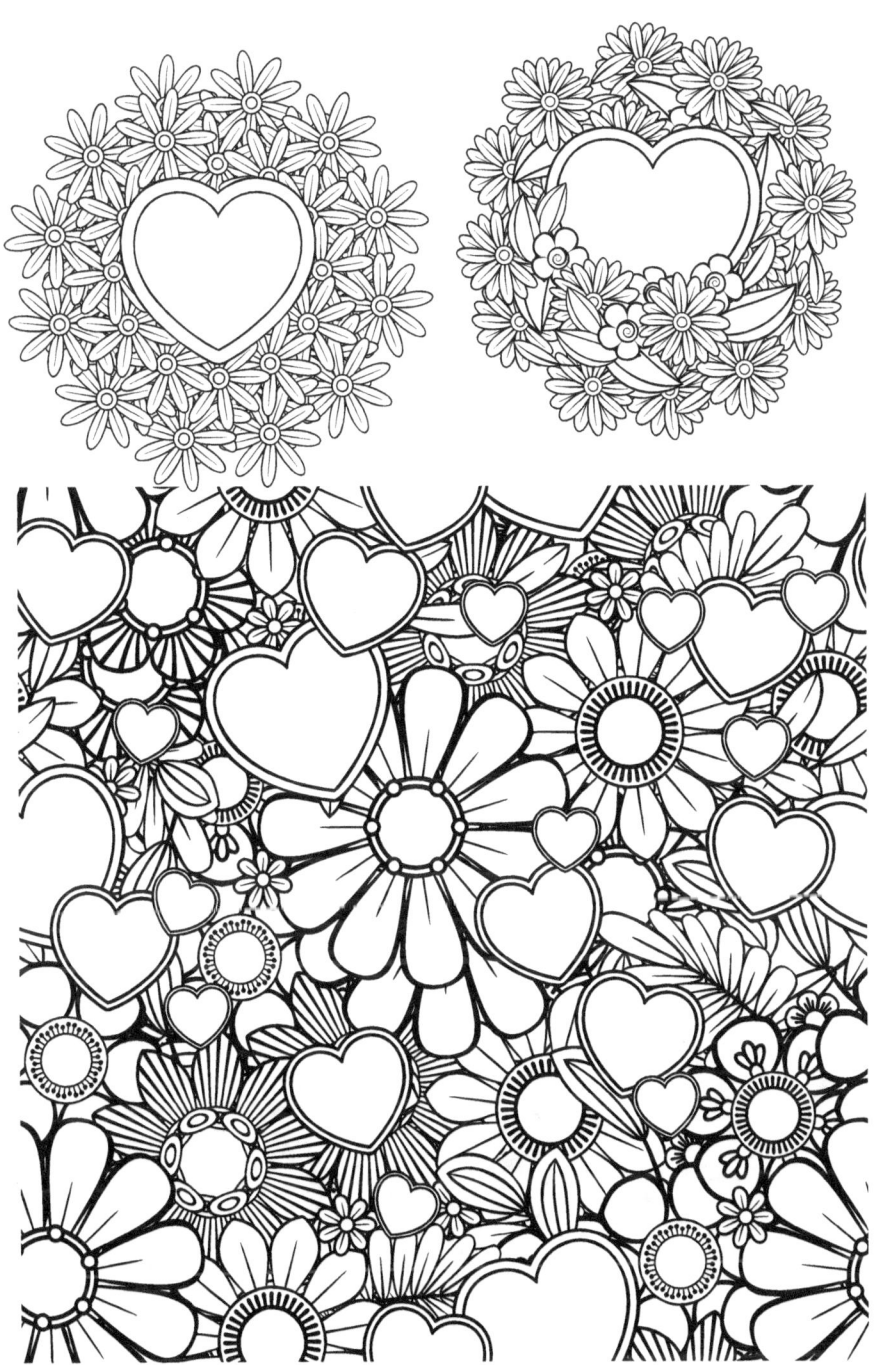

How do ants start their workday? With an
"introduction to the bee"!

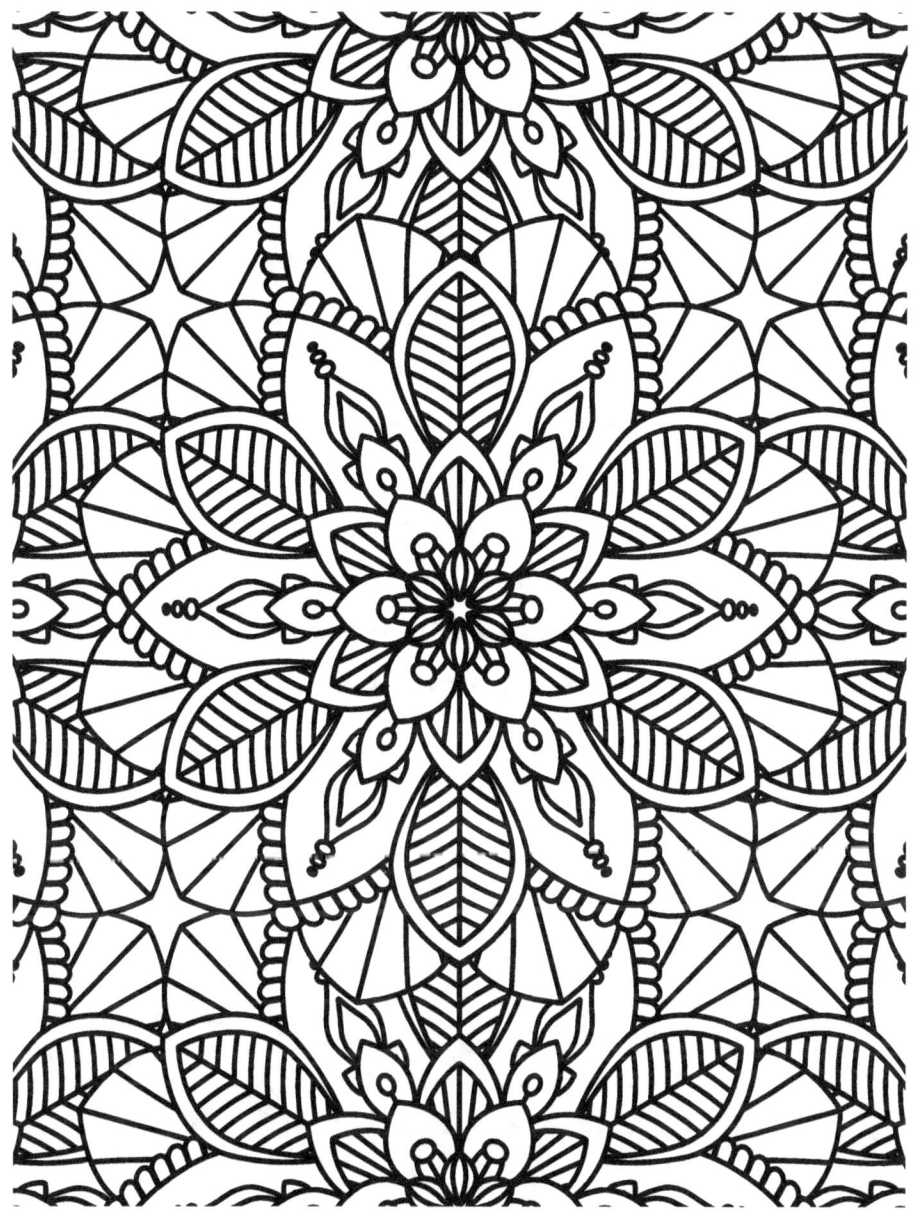

Smiles and laughter echoed through the petals, and the sweet aroma of nectar drew butterflies and bees into a dance of joy and harmony. Those who looked at this wonderful garden felt surrounded by beauty and peace, and every corner hid a secret, a story of a flower that had found its place in everyone's hearts. This is how our story ended, but in each colorful flower hides a new adventure, a new coloring page and a lot of relaxation after a day's work

this coloring book has been created by
clau_criss

I hope you enjoyed the jokes and that
I succeeded in making your day better

www.ingramcontent.com/pod-product-compliance
Lightning Source LLC
Chambersburg PA
CBHW070805290526
45795CB00002B/633